UNDERSTANDING
RICHARD RUSSO

UNDERSTANDING CONTEMPORARY AMERICAN LITERATURE
Matthew J. Bruccoli, Founding Editor
Linda Wagner-Martin, Series Editor

Volumes on

Edward Albee | Sherman Alexie | Nelson Algren | Paul Auster
Nicholson Baker | John Barth | Donald Barthelme | The Beats
Thomas Berger | The Black Mountain Poets | Robert Bly | T. C. Boyle
Truman Capote | Raymond Carver | Michael Chabon | Fred Chappell
Chicano Literature | Contemporary American Drama
Contemporary American Horror Fiction
Contemporary American Literary Theory
Contemporary American Science Fiction, 1926–1970
Contemporary American Science Fiction, 1970–2000
Contemporary Chicana Literature | Robert Coover | Philip K. Dick
James Dickey | E. L. Doctorow | Rita Dove | John Gardner | George Garrett
Tim Gautreaux | John Hawkes | Joseph Heller | Lillian Hellman | Beth Henley
James Leo Herlihy | David Henry Hwang | John Irving | Randall Jarrell
Charles Johnson | Diane Johnson | Adrienne Kennedy | William Kennedy
Jack Kerouac | Jamaica Kincaid | Etheridge Knight | Tony Kushner
Ursula K. Le Guin | Denise Levertov | Bernard Malamud | David Mamet
Bobbie Ann Mason | Colum McCann | Cormac McCarthy | Jill McCorkle
Carson McCullers | W. S. Merwin | Arthur Miller | Stephen Millhauser
Lorrie Moore | Toni Morrison's Fiction | Vladimir Nabokov | Gloria Naylor
Joyce Carol Oates | Tim O'Brien | Flannery O'Connor | Cynthia Ozick
Suzan-Lori Parks | Walker Percy | Katherine Anne Porter | Richard Powers
Reynolds Price | Annie Proulx | Thomas Pynchon | Theodore Roethke
Philip Roth | Richard Russo | May Sarton | Hubert Selby, Jr. | Mary Lee Settle
Sam Shepard | Neil Simon | Isaac Bashevis Singer | Jane Smiley | Gary Snyder
William Stafford | Robert Stone | Anne Tyler | Gerald Vizenor | Kurt Vonnegut
David Foster Wallace | Robert Penn Warren | James Welch | Eudora Welty
Edmund White | Tennessee Williams | August Wilson | Charles Wright

UNDERSTANDING

RICHARD RUSSO

Kathleen Drowne

The University of South Carolina Press

© 2014 University of South Carolina

Published by the University of South Carolina Press
Columbia, South Carolina 29208

www.sc.edu/uscpress

Manufactured in the United States of America

23 22 21 20 19 18 17 16 15 14   10 9 8 7 6 5 4 3 2 1

Library of Congress Cataloging-in-Publication Data

Drowne, Kathleen Morgan.
  Understanding Richard Russo / Kathleen Drowne.
    pages cm. — (Understanding contemporary American literature)
  Includes bibliographical references and index.
    ISBN 978-1-61117-402-1 (hardbound : alk. paper) — ISBN 978-1-61117-403-8
(ebook) 1. Russo, Richard, 1949– —Interpretation and criticism.
2. Russo, Richard, 1949– —Biography. 3. Working class in literature.
I. Title.
  PS3568.U812Z58 2014
  813'.54—dc23

                                                  2014007292

For Patrick, Genevieve, and William

CONTENTS

SERIES EDITOR'S PREFACE

The Understanding Contemporary American Literature series was founded by the estimable Matthew J. Bruccoli (1931–2008), who envisioned these volumes as guides or companions for students as well as good nonacademic readers, a legacy that will continue as new volumes are developed to fill in gaps among the nearly one hundred series volumes published to date and to embrace a host of new writers only now making their marks on our literature.

As Professor Bruccoli explained in his preface to the volumes he edited, because much influential contemporary literature makes special demands, "the word 'understanding' in the titles was chosen deliberately. Many willing readers lack an adequate understanding of how contemporary literature works; that is, of what the author is attempting to express and the means by which it is conveyed." Aimed at fostering this understanding of good literature and good writers, the criticism and analyses in the series provide instruction in how to read certain contemporary writers—explicating their material, language, structures, themes, and perspectives—and facilitate a more profitable experience of the works under discussion.

In the twenty-first century Professor Bruccoli's prescience gives us an avenue to publish expert critiques of significant contemporary American writing. The series continues to map the literary landscape and to provide both instruction and enjoyment. Future volumes will seek to introduce new voices alongside canonized favorites, to chronicle the changing literature of our times, and to remain, as Professor Bruccoli conceived, contemporary in the best sense of the word.

Linda Wagner-Martin, Series Editor

ACKNOWLEDGMENTS

I would like to thank several people whose assistance made this book possible. The librarians at the Curtis Laws Wilson Library at the Missouri University of Science and Technology, especially Dawn Mick, Marsha Fuller, and June Snell, cheerfully helped me acquire dozens of items that contributed to this work. My research assistant, Samantha Dean, tracked down many interviews with Richard Russo that I might not have been able to find otherwise. Dr. Kristine Swenson, my department chair and a good friend, was supportive and unfailingly optimistic throughout the process. Linda Wagner-Martin was infinitely more patient with me than I deserved.

Richard Russo was kind enough to answer my questions and offer his support of the project, and he sent me a very helpful advance copy of *Elsewhere*. I am grateful for his generosity and hope that he continues to produce his poignant, honest, big-hearted novels for many years to come.

Most of all I thank—and am thankful for—Patrick, Genevieve, and William, who have supported and encouraged my work from the very beginning. Only they know how much I owe them, and only I know how much they have blessed my life.

CHAPTER 1

Understanding Richard Russo

> The thing that I would say about literature in general, the thing that I
> love most about it, is that when I'm in the world of a gifted writer I'm
> able to see that world through that writer's eyes, not my own.
>
> —Richard Russo, interview with Robert Birnbaum, *Identity Theory*

In the introduction to *The Story Behind the Story* (2004), an anthology of
short fiction that includes authors' explanations of how their stories came
about, Richard Russo recalls the countless times he has been asked if he
thinks writing can be taught or if writers are just "born this way."[1] Such
questioners, Russo posits, seem to be asking if some innate difference sepa-
rates writers from nonwriters or if we all start out essentially the same. Russo
responds to this question with a bit of a dodge: "The unsatisfactory truth of
the matter—and most readers suspect this—is that we're both the same *and*
different" (10). Perhaps fittingly, this paradoxical concept of being simultaneously the same and different pervades Russo's body of work at many levels,
particularly concerning his position as a successful writer doggedly reckoning
with his experiences growing up in the small industrial town of Gloversville,
New York. In many ways Russo is the same as the men and women who
live and work in the circumscribed environment of a Rust Belt factory town,
struggling to support their families and build satisfying lives; he was raised
among leather workers and understands intimately the frustrations and joys
of life in a close-knit, dead-end community. Yet he is also undeniably different. As a young man, Russo fled Gloversville for college in Arizona, rarely
returning after his graduation, and created for himself a life indelibly colored
by his past but not exclusively defined by it. He can write about small-town,
working-class men and women in fictional towns such as Mohawk, North

Bath, Empire Falls, and Thomaston because he knows, authentically, what their lives are like. At the same time, his many years away from Gloversville, living and working in college towns all over the United States, give him a personal and narrative perspective that is undeniably different from those of the folks he left behind. He is truly both the same and different from the people who filled his childhood and who populate his novels.

James Richard Russo was born in Johnstown, New York, on July 15, 1949, the only child of James W. "Jimmy" Russo and Jean Findlay (LeVarn) Russo. He grew up in the nearby town of Gloversville, which was known during the late nineteenth and early twentieth centuries for its production of fine leather goods, particularly gloves. Russo's maternal grandfather was a glove cutter who moved to Gloversville from Vermont, and his paternal grandfather, a shoemaker in Italy, immigrated to Gloversville in order to join the industrial boom that the town was then enjoying, but unfortunately would not enjoy for much longer. Russo's father, a World War II army veteran, worked part-time as a glove cutter until he was laid off. He began drinking heavily and left his family when his son was very young; from that point he made his living working on road construction crews.[2] Russo's mother worked first as a telephone operator and then at General Electric's computer room in Schenectady, an hour's commute from Gloversville, "loading and unloading large wheel-like tape drives onto a computer the size of a bus."[3] As a single mother, Jean Russo attempted to maintain a certain level of independence, but she did rely heavily on her parents and then, later, on her son for both financial and emotional support.

Russo grew up in a modest but comfortable two-family house on Helwig Street in Gloversville owned by his maternal grandparents, with whom he was close. His grandparents lived in the two-bedroom, one-bathroom apartment on the first floor, and he and his mother shared the upstairs, identical apartment. Russo fondly remembers his grandfather, a veteran of both world wars, who suffered and died from emphysema no doubt caused, at least in part, by the dusty, toxic rooms where he worked cutting leather for gloves. But, as Russo recounts, his grandfather never held the tanneries responsible for his illness and instead maintained that despite the dangerous conditions of the factories, "the glove shops had put bread on his family's table for all those years, and what would he have done, how would he otherwise have made a living?"[4] His grandfather's somewhat surprising sense of appreciation for the tanneries echoes in several of Russo's novels, especially his first, *Mohawk,* in which an elderly former tannery worker makes a similar claim: the workingmen *needed* those shops, and their utter reliance on the tanneries for their livelihood trumped any impulse they might have to criticize their poor working conditions or blame them for the town's shockingly high cancer rates.

The young Russo served as an altar boy at Sacred Heart Church and spent many Saturday afternoons at the movies shown at the Glove Theater in downtown Gloversville.[5] He spent his boyhood "happy as a clam," playing baseball and basketball with his friends and cousins, and earning spending money by raking leaves in the fall, shoveling snow in the winter, and mowing lawns in the summer.[6] Although Russo grew up in a community deeply connected to the leather industry, he never actually worked in the tanneries. His grandfather, father, uncle, and cousins, however, held various jobs in the leather shops, including in the beam house, doing "the wettest, foulest, lowest-paid, and most dangerous work in the whole tannery,"[7] and their experiences provided Russo with lasting insight into the daily lives of tannery workers. While he was a college student, Russo returned in the summers to Gloversville, where he worked alongside his father doing backbreaking road construction work. Despite the grueling physical challenges of the job, he recalls being tempted to forgo higher education and instead stay on the road crew with his father "to do that hard, honest work that he and his friends did all year round."[8] Like Ned Hall in *The Risk Pool* and Nate Wilson in *Nate in Venice,* Russo recognized and appreciated that hard physical labor had an appeal unlike that of intellectual work but nearly as powerful. Nevertheless he chose the path of education and left his days on the road crew, and among the leatherworkers of Gloversville, behind him.

Russo's mother, like several of the mothers in his fiction (most notably Grace Roby in *Empire Falls*), dreamed of sending her son away from Gloversville and toward a life beyond its conscripted boundaries. So, unlike his college-bound classmates who chose to attend area universities, Russo headed for the University of Arizona in Tucson in the fall of 1967, after his graduation from Bishop Burke High School. His mother accompanied him to Arizona and settled in nearby Phoenix, where she landed a new job and temporarily put her Gloversville life behind her. The two of them drove to Arizona together in his decrepit 1960 Ford Galaxie, nicknamed "the Gray Death," towing a U-Haul trailer behind. Russo took a B.A. in English in 1971, a Ph.D. in English in 1980, and an M.F.A. in 1981. His two advanced degrees coincided because, as Russo has explained in interviews, he became stalled while writing his doctoral dissertation about the early American novelist Charles Brockden Brown and began to feel himself losing interest in writing about other books.[9] He started to perceive the work of literary scholarship as fundamentally antithetical to his love of literature. As he explained to one interviewer in 2010, "By the time I'd finished my course work and was starting to write my dissertation, I was in a pit of despair. I realized I'd made a terrible mistake that was going to affect and infect the rest of my life. I could see absolutely no way out of it, until I discovered creative writing. I discovered that, in doing all of that reading, I was studying to be a writer. Creative writing gave me another avenue, and it saved my life."[10] Russo did manage to persevere and complete his dissertation, but even as he continued to meet the expectations of his Ph.D. program, he began to write short stories and to work on a novel. Ultimately he earned an M.F.A. degree on the strength of these stories, several of which were published in literary magazines shortly after his graduation.

While still a student at Arizona, he met Barbara Young; they married in 1972, moved into a single-wide trailer on the outskirts of Tucson, and struggled to scrape together a living. Barbara worked a nine-to-five job in her father's failing electronics firm while Russo continued his graduate work, taught classes at the University of Arizona, and on weekends sang in a popular restaurant. After graduation he worked for a year as a visiting assistant professor at Arizona State University, and then accepted a position as an assistant professor of English at Penn State–Altoona. In 1984 the Russos left Pennsylvania for Southern Connecticut State University in New Haven, where Richard took a position as an assistant professor. He described this period of his life as a "decadelong academic nomadship" during which he was simultaneously teaching and writing, seeking jobs that offered him more time to write even if they offered lower salaries.[11] Throughout these years Russo was publishing short stories in literary journals, and many of these stories harbored the seeds of future novels. For example, "The Top of the Tree," which appeared in the first issue of the *Mid-American Review* in 1981, includes a tree-climbing boy with an absent father and a needy mother—a scenario that resurfaces, in modified form, in *The Risk Pool*.

After selling his first novel, *Mohawk*, in 1986, Russo and his family—which now included two young daughters—moved to Carbondale, Illinois, where he had been offered a position in the writing program at Southern Illinois University. The Russo family stayed in Carbondale for five years, during which time Russo's writing career began to blossom. After the considerable success of *Mohawk*, Russo released *The Risk Pool* (1988), also set in the town of Mohawk, and began work on his next two novels. In 1991 he and his family moved again, this time to Waterville, Maine, so Russo could accept a part-time position at Colby College that allowed him much more time to write. He remained on the faculty there until he retired from teaching, around 1995, to focus on his writing full-time.

In 1993 Russo extended his examination of difficult father-son relationships begun in *Mohawk* and *The Risk Pool* when he released *Nobody's Fool*, the story of the Sullivan family's four generations of misfits and failures. Set in North Bath, a declining hamlet in upstate New York, the novel centers on Donald "Sully" Sullivan, the "nobody's fool" of the title. His warm, caring relationship with his grandson Will provides Sully the strength to confront memories of his abusive father and, eventually, to mend relations with his son and many of his fellow townspeople. In 1994 the novel was made into a feature film starring Paul Newman, Jessica Tandy, Bruce Willis, and Melanie Griffith. In 1997 Russo followed up with *Straight Man,* a marked departure from his first three novels. *Straight Man* is an academic satire set in rural Pennsylvania at a university partly based on Penn State–Altoona, where Russo briefly taught. The protagonist, Hank Devereaux, is a marginal English professor at a nondescript, regional state university who is elected interim chair of the department because he is considered too incompetent to upset the tenuous equilibrium among the subpar but mostly tenured faculty. He surprises everyone, however, when he assumes leadership (through unconventional means) and attempts to rescue his colleagues' jobs, which are threatened by draconian administrative budget cuts.

In 2001 Russo released *Empire Falls*, which won the Pulitzer Prize for fiction in 2002. The novel, set in the fictional town of Empire Falls, Maine, but loosely based on the real towns of Skowhegan and Waterville, Maine, and Gloversville, New York, encompasses several generations and dozens of characters in a sweeping narrative about life in a dead-end mill town. The protagonist, Miles Roby, is perhaps one of Russo's most endearing characters; humble and hardworking, he struggles to stay connected to his teenage daughter, Tick, and to understand—and at points even transcend—the modest expectations of his small-town life. Russo also wrote the teleplay for a two-part miniseries based on the novel, which aired on HBO in 2005 and starred Paul Newman, Ed Harris, Helen Hunt, and Philip Seymour Hoffman. In a 2008 interview, Russo recounted his tremendous surprise that *Empire Falls,* which had not been shortlisted for any major prizes, captured the Pulitzer. He commented, "I fully expect one morning to wake up and get a telephone call from someone telling me: 'We are terribly sorry. We have been recalculating the 2002 Pulitzer and we're sorry to have to say you didn't win after all.'"[12]

Russo followed the successful *Empire Falls* with his first collection of short fiction, *The Whore's Child,* in 2002. The title story, which examines the experiences of a creative writing professor who encounters an elderly nun determined to tell her life story, was featured as the Boston Book Festival's "One City One Story" choice in 2011. Reviews of *The Whore's Child* were largely positive, and many critics noted that while Russo's short fiction tends to be less humorous than his long novels, in them he gravitates toward many of the same themes that dominate his longer works. In one piece, "Poison," two writers from the same working-class mill town reveal very different understandings of and relationships with their pasts. Several others, including "The Farther You Go," "Monhegan Light," and "Buoyancy," contend with failed or unhappy marriages. One reviewer noted that even though the principal characters in *The Whore's Child* tend to be writers or artists, "their concerns are not so different from the blue-collar folk of *Nobody's Fool* or *Empire Falls:* the advance of age; the fleeting joys and inevitable complications of love, marriage, and children."[13]

In 2007 Russo released *Bridge of Sighs,* his longest and most interior novel to date. Like *Mohawk, The Risk Pool, Nobody's Fool,* and *Empire Falls,* this novel takes place in a small, defunct backwater town with a distinct class system firmly in place and a powerful nostalgia for the good old days of industry and prosperity that clouds the not-so-prosperous present. In *Bridge of Sighs* the narrative attention is divided between three primary characters. Lou C. "Lucy" Lynch, a shopkeeper born and raised in Thomaston, New York, loves his town and sees no reason ever to leave. In contrast, Bobby Marconi, Lucy's childhood friend, flees Thomaston after high school, changes his name to Robert Noonan, and becomes a famous painter in Venice. Sarah, who loves both and is loved by both, marries Lou but never stops wondering what that choice has meant to her life. The darkest of all Russo's novels, *Bridge of Sighs* spins out these characters' epic emotional journeys that transcend geographic limitations.

Two years after *Bridge of Sighs,* Russo published his seventh novel, *That Old Cape Magic* (2009). Far shorter and much funnier than *Bridge of Sighs, That Old Cape Magic* takes as its focus not the denizens of decrepit manufacturing towns such as Mohawk or Empire Falls but rather Jack Griffin, a college professor and sometime screenwriter who wrestles, with varying success, to come to terms with the legacies of his deceased academic parents. Along the way Griffin must negotiate his deteriorating marriage, his insufferable in-laws, and his only daughter's wedding. Although the story is punctuated with moments of overt and sometimes slapstick humor, *That Old Cape Magic* also offers a serious examination of the complexities of family relationships, middle-age crises of confidence, and questions about the true nature of happiness.

Recently, Russo has ventured into new literary territory. His two major works published in 2012 dramatically depart from his previous patterns of long narration and gradual development of character ensembles. The first, *Interventions,* is a collection of four short pieces, each published as a separate booklet and collected in a single slipcase, that Russo calls "a tribute to the printed word." Each of the four works, "Intervention," "The Whore's Child," "High and Dry," and "Horseman," is accompanied by a color print of an original illustration by Russo's younger daughter, the artist Kate Russo. The longest of the pieces, "Intervention," is a previously unpublished novella. "The Whore's Child" is, of course, the title piece in Russo's short-story collection of 2002. "High and Dry" appeared in *Granta* in 2010, and "Horseman" was first published in the *Atlantic* fiction issue in 2006. To underscore Russo's commitment to print publishing, *Interventions* was released only in paper form and was published by Down East Books, a small press in Camden, Maine, where Russo used to live part-time. In a *Publishers Weekly* interview, Kate Russo explained, "We wanted to do something anti-Kindle. We wanted it to be sustainable, and printed in the U.S. Sort of in the theme of 'High and Dry.' Don't outsource what you don't need to."[14] Richard Russo has acknowledged that *Interventions* may challenge would-be readers with its suggested list price of forty dollars, noting, "It's more money than people are used to paying not only for Richard Russo novels but for books since Amazon began driving down the price."[15]

Russo's second major publication in 2012, *Elsewhere,* is described on its cover as a memoir but focuses far more closely on Russo's mother than on the writer himself. Jean Russo, who died in 2007, apparently suffered for much of her life from undiagnosed obsessive-compulsive disorder; her erratic and often irrational behaviors posed many challenges for her only son, who as an adult spent much of his time and attention caring for her. Early on, Jean established that she and her son were a "team," and henceforth they were rarely separated for long periods of time. Both funny and poignant, *Elsewhere* serves as Russo's tribute to his mother's unshakable belief in her own independence (even when she fell far short of this mark) as well as an honest examination of the ways that his mother's intensifying needs clashed with his own goals of becoming a writer, a husband, and a father.

Early in 2013 Russo added to his growing list of publications with the novella *Nate in Venice,* published by byliner.com exclusively as a digital book and available on the byliner.com Web site, as a Kindle Single, and through the iTunes store. Aware of the difficulties of publishing novellas through traditional channels and yet being a longtime fan of the form, Russo eagerly

explored the option of releasing his novella as an e-book. Despite the nontraditional format, *Nate in Venice* returns to several familiar themes in Russo's
oeuvre, specifically the aging male protagonist facing regrets about the decisions he has made, the relationships he has damaged, and the life he has
chosen. Nonetheless, *Nate in Venice* is not a bleak story; Russo's trademark
humor and warmth shine through even the darkest parts of the story, and
ultimately Nate finds the will to face his future with a real sense of hope.

Throughout his professional life, Russo has contributed introductions,
prefaces, and chapters to multiple collections of fiction and nonfiction. He
edited *A Healing Touch: True Stories of Life, Death, and Hospice* (2008),
to which he also contributed a poignant essay about a friend's wife who suffered from Alzheimer's disease. Down East Books released *A Healing Touch,*
and all the royalties, along with a portion of the publisher's profits, were dedicated to a hospice organization in rural Maine. Russo also edited and wrote
the introduction to the 2010 edition of *The Best American Short Stories,* the
introduction to *The Collected Stories of Richard Yates* (2001), and the foreword for *Bottom of the Ninth: Great Contemporary Baseball Short Stories*
(2003). He contributed essays on the craft of writing to *Creating Fiction:
Instruction and Insights from Teachers of the Associated Writing Programs*
(1999), *Bringing the Devil to His Knees: The Craft of Fiction and the Writing
Life* (2001), and *The Story Behind the Story: 26 Stories by Contemporary
Writers and How They Work* (2004). He has published two humorous essays about food: "Pork," in *We Are What We Ate: 24 Memories of Food*
(1998); and "Surf and Turf," in *Death by Pad Thai and Other Unforgettable
Meals* (2006). He wrote the introduction to *My Bookstore: Writers Celebrate
Their Favorite Places to Browse, Read, and Shop* (2012) and contributed to
a documentary film and book of interviews titled *Scout, Atticus, and Boo: A
Celebration of Fifty Years of* To Kill a Mockingbird (2010). He also wrote
a long afterword for *She's Not There: A Life in Two Genders* (2003), by
Jennifer Finney Boylan. Boylan, a transgendered woman, was Russo's best
friend and office mate at Colby College before she transitioned, and although
Russo struggled at first to come to terms with his friend's gender transformation, the two have remained close. Russo is featured in *She's Not There,* and
his afterword, which details some of the personal challenges he faced as he
witnessed his outwardly male friend changing to a female identity, includes
some of Russo's most poignant and honest autobiographical writing.

Russo has also enjoyed considerable success writing screenplays for
Hollywood films and television movies. He cowrote the screenplay for *Twi-
light* (1998) with the director Robert Benton, who adapted Russo's *Nobody's
Fool* into a 1994 Paramount film that he also directed. Russo also wrote the

teleplay for the Hallmark channel's *The Flamingo Rising,* a drama starring William Hurt, which aired in 2001, and *Brush with Fate* (2003), starring Glenn Close, also for the Hallmark channel. In 2005 he adapted *Empire Falls,* his Pulitzer Prize–winning novel, into a teleplay for HBO; the miniseries garnered an Emmy and two Golden Globe awards. He and Benton cowrote the screenplay for *The Ice Harvest* (2005), a dark comedy-drama directed by Harold Ramis and starring John Cusack. Along with the director Niall Johnson, Russo cowrote the screenplay for *Keeping Mum* (2005), a comedy starring Rowan Atkinson, Kristin Scott Thomas, and Maggie Smith. Russo has frequently commented on his screenwriting in interviews, noting that he enjoys the work and that "writing screenplays plays right into my strengths, because most screenplays are about dialogue, which comes easiest for me." He also admits that he loves returning to novels after a screenplay is finished, because "it feels like I've been working with a hammer and a wrench . . . and when I start on a novel again, it's like I take out my old tool box. I've only been using a couple of tools, and then I flip it up and look at all those things in there that you use when you write a novel; it's good to be able to use all those tools again."[16]

In 1999 the Russos bought a restored nineteenth-century home in Camden, a small town on the coast of Maine. For several years the couple divided their time between their Camden home and a renovated condominium in Boston's old downtown Leather District, a connection that hearkened back to Russo's roots in the leather town of Gloversville. In late 2012 the Russos moved permanently to Portland, Maine. Richard continues to write full-time, and Barbara works as a realtor in the Portland market.

Influences and Narrative Style

In a 2010 interview, Richard Russo explained that even though his Ph.D. in American literature did not lead to a traditional academic career, studying literature helped him develop into a creative writer. He read voraciously while a student but never felt drawn to many of the postmodern, metafictional novelists whom his colleagues admired. Rather his graduate school experience led him to understand that he was "the kind of writer who was informed by Dickens, the Brontës, and Twain." Along with those iconic nineteenth-century writers, he also began seeking out more traditional contemporary writers who "had a sensibility closer to my own,"[17] such as Richard Yates, John Cheever, and Alice Munro.

Although Russo professes a deep affinity for these more recent American writers, he chooses not to pattern his writing after theirs. Still, his admiration for Yates's work emanates throughout his thoughtful introduction to *The*

Collected Stories of Richard Yates (2001), in which he claims that "the excitement one feels reading these dark stories, I believe, is the exhilaration of encountering, recognizing, and embracing the truth" and that, more bleakly, we "recognize ourselves in the blindness, the neediness, the loneliness, even the cruelty of Yates's people."[18] Russo's work, though, is inherently more optimistic than Yates's and far funnier. As Russo noted in a 2001 interview, the characters in Yates's work "go from bad trouble to worse trouble and end up in heartbreak the way moths go to flames. In very few of his stories is he ever able to achieve the kind of marginal hope that I arrive at in just about everything I write."[19]

According to Russo, few of his favorite books were written in the last half-century or even the last century. In interviews he has frequently named Charles Dickens as his most important literary influence and *Great Expectations* among his favorite novels, although he acknowledged that he loves "all of Dickens, really. The breadth of his canvas, the importance he places on minor characters, his understanding that comedy is serious business. And in the character of Pip [from *Great Expectations*], I learned, even before I understood I'd learned it, that we recognize ourselves in a character's weakness as much as his strength."[20] Indeed it is easy to see Dickens's influence on Russo's novels, most of which feature large casts of characters and meandering plots that wind in and out of dozens of intersecting lives. In particular, *Empire Falls* and *Bridge of Sighs* focus on central characters who come of age in colorful and tightly knit (albeit somewhat dysfunctional) communities not unlike Pip's world in *Great Expectations*. Although critics have sometimes complained about the extensive length and slow pace of Russo's novels, he remains unapologetically loyal to Dickensian strategies of storytelling, noting that character development takes time and that great stories can be built on deeply wrought characters and not just swift plotlines.

Russo has frequently invoked Dickens in interviews as well as in his nonfiction writing, often in unexpected contexts, and clearly presumed that his readers would understand his allusions. For example, in the foreword to *Bottom of the Ninth: Great Contemporary Baseball Stories*, edited by Russo's friend, colleague, and former student John McNally, Russo manages to slip in a Dickens comparison in his comment that "the astute reader will quickly note that most of these stories are not really about baseball, but baseball creeps into them, like King Charles's head into Mr. Dick's memoir in *David Copperfield*" (xiii). As another example, in an interview about *To Kill a Mockingbird*, which aired as part of a 2010 documentary titled *Scout, Atticus, and Boo* and was published in book form under the same title, Russo draws Dickens into his comments about Harper Lee's iconic novel. He notes

that "there was something about the opening of *Great Expectations* that bur-
rowed very, very deep [in me]. *To Kill a Mockingbird* was that way" (168).

Russo identifies Mark Twain's *The Adventures of Huckleberry Finn* as
another novel that has influenced his work in important ways, insofar as it
taught him that "you can put bigotry, ignorance, violence, every part of the
American character that we wish weren't there, all the things that make us
cringe—you can go there if you go armed with humor. If you don't you're
going to find people putting down your book."[21] He also admires F. Scott
Fitzgerald's *The Great Gatsby*, in part because of its timeless concerns with
"class, money, [and] the invention of self [that] are so central to the American
experience."[22] Indeed one is hard-pressed to think of any piece of Russo's
fiction that does not contend, at least in some capacity, with issues of class,
the invention of the self, or both.

Like Dickens and Twain as well as another favorite, John Steinbeck,
Russo gravitates toward the omniscient point of view in his fiction. He makes
a convincing case for employing omniscient narrators in his essay "In Defense of Omniscience," his contribution to the collection *Bringing the Devil
to His Knees* (2001). In this essay Russo argues that omniscience is "a mature
writer's technique" that "has something to do with years, with experience
of life, with the gradual accumulation of knowledge and pain and wisdom.
Omniscience not only invents a world; it tells us how that world works and
how we should feel about the way it works."[23] Allegations that omniscient
narration is an old-fashioned technique seem to Russo irrelevant. "Well, gentle reader, who gives a damn?" he responds. "Are we talking old-fashioned
in the sense of being part of an extended, rich literary tradition? There are
worse things."[24] The nature of Russo's omniscient narration, however, varies
from novel to novel. He uses close third-person omniscient narration in *Empire Falls* and *That Old Cape Magic*, more universal omniscience in *Mohawk*
and *Nobody's Fool*, and a complicated but effective blend of first-person and
third-person omniscience in *Bridge of Sighs*. Straight first-person narrators
tell the stories in *The Risk Pool* and *Straight Man*, often to great comic effect. Always we as readers are privy to the internal musings of at least one
central character, and in many cases we can witness the thoughts of several
important players in the tale.

Major Themes

The element of Richard Russo's work perhaps most often noted by critics
is his genuine and abiding affection for the ordinary, small-town, working-
class characters who populate his fiction. These characters are often down-
at-the-heels, unemployed or underemployed, beset by economic and familial

pressures, and saddled with histories of making questionable decisions. Although they reside in crumbling manufacturing towns where most of the jobs have left, many of the workers doggedly remain while scrambling to eke out livings amid boarded-up factories and deserted downtowns. Nevertheless these men (they are almost always men) often behave admirably—even nobly—and Russo depicts them with generosity, respect, and good humor. His fondness for such characters and his honest depiction of them have led critics to describe Russo as a "bard of the working class," a kind of spokesperson for those without much education, money, or future prospects. Indeed many of Russo's working-class characters, including Sully in *Nobody's Fool,* Sam Hall in *The Risk Pool,* Miles Roby in *Empire Falls,* and Big Lou Lynch in *Bridge of Sighs,* appear as quiet heroes despite their many flaws and shortcomings. Their often clumsy and frequently ineffectual attempts to do the right thing, even when they misjudge what the right thing actually is, generate powerful empathy and identification among readers.

The empathy that Russo creates for his protagonists is amplified by the careful detail with which he presents their surroundings. The dying towns of Mohawk, North Bath, Thomaston, and Empire Falls take on a kind of dignity through Russo's prose; his bleak depictions of empty factories, decaying neighborhoods, and blighted downtowns are humanized through his compassionate portrayals of the residents and workers who still reside and work (or used to work) in these locations. Russo's ability to bring to life these struggling small towns left behind by the global economy has led readers and critics alike to think of him as a writer focused primarily on place. Russo has commented on his contribution to a rural American literary tradition anchored by Sherwood Anderson's seminal short-story cycle *Winesburg, Ohio* (1919). In a 2009 interview Russo explained, "When I first started writing my small mill town novels, I definitely felt like I was part of a tradition. For me, the book was *Winesburg, Ohio,* and this is still an enormously important book, much more than Sinclair Lewis, who was also doing small town books. Sinclair Lewis was so down the nose about it; whereas in *Winesburg, Ohio,* you get the feeling that Sherwood Anderson was writing about people's lives that were every bit as rich, multi-dimensional, full of the same dreams, fears and anxieties as big city people."[25] Indeed, Russo's fiction reveals a profound respect for his realistic but highly eccentric small-town characters—worn-out shopkeepers, mill workers, and odd-jobbers, alcoholics, invalids, reprobates, and ne'er-do-wells—whose tragicomic lives represent both the dignity and the desperation he sees in crumbling Rust Belt towns.

Although Russo might justifiably be deemed a great chronicler of American small towns, his attention to place is actually more of a by-product of his even greater attention to socioeconomic class. His characters represent a particular stratum of the American class system, and their lives reflect not only the vagaries and peculiarities of a particular town in a particular region but also the strategies that the working class enacts to survive in environments that offer few options for employment and even fewer opportunities for advancement. With only a handful of exceptions (including Hank Devereaux in *Straight Man* and Jack Griffin in *That Old Cape Magic*, who are both professors), Russo's characters tend to have jobs, not careers. They work with their hands and their backs, not their minds, in tanneries, on road crews, in diners and convenience stores. They deliver milk, paint houses, and hang Sheetrock. They endure seasonal layoffs and long weeks with no paychecks; they ask their friends for loans during rough patches and offer loans when they are flush. Characters such as Sam Hall (*The Risk Pool*) and Sully (*Nobody's Fool*) in particular live close to the edge: no savings, no insurance, no safety net. It is to this environment that Russo gravitates. Russo spent much of his adult life as a university professor, and his familiarity with academic types runs deep. Interestingly his academic characters, Henry Devereaux and Jack Griffin, are true narcissists who, although they mean well, can never stop thinking about themselves and their needs. In stark contrast are Russo's many working-class characters who, with only a few exceptions, demonstrate true kindness, selflessness, and generosity of spirit.

Along with Russo's reputation for place-based and class-based fiction, critics have also frequently commented on the centrality of family relationships in his fiction, particularly the often tense dynamic between parents and children. *Mohawk* certainly includes its share of such complicated and sometimes badly damaged relationships, but it is now clear that at this early stage in his career Russo was merely warming up. His second novel, *The Risk Pool*, is dedicated to his father, and in it Russo admits to working out, through the fictional story of Sam and Ned Hall, elements of the fractured relationship he had with his own often-absent father. Dysfunctional father-son relationships also dominate Russo's next novel, *Nobody's Fool*, and are amplified by the multigenerational elements of the fractures. Donald "Sully" Sullivan struggles to come to terms with the abuse he suffered at the hands of his own drunken, abusive father, even as he tries to justify his own abandonment of his son, Peter. Much atonement and redemption exist in this novel, though, and Sully's genuine connection to his grandson helps him reconnect with Peter and even accept, in a way, his feelings toward his late father.

Russo is not finished with fathers and sons, though, not by a long shot. *Empire Falls* presents Miles Roby's complicated and frustrating relationship with his father, Max, though it also shows the tender and compassionate devotion that Miles feels toward his teenage daughter, Tick. *Straight Man* presents Hank Devereaux's thorny relationship with his father, a successful academic but a complete failure as a family man. *Bridge of Sighs* portrays the complete devotion of one son toward his father, who may not have deserved such worship, and the complete antagonism of another son toward his father, who might have deserved better. *That Old Cape Magic*, like *Straight Man*, points us again toward an academic son in pointless and frustrating competition with an academic father.

None of Russo's novels lacks a problematic father-son relationship, though it must be acknowledged that mothers and sons also experience their share of conflict. In *Mohawk*, Anne Grouse struggles with her relationships with both her father and her son. *The Risk Pool*'s Ned and Jenny Hall abandon all honesty in their dealings with one another. Multiple other pairs of mothers and sons clash almost fanatically with one another (Peter and Vera in *Nobody's Fool*; Lucy and Tessa in *Bridge of Sighs*; Griffin and Mary in *That Old Cape Magic*; and, of course, Russo and his own mother, Jean, as explained in his memoir, *Elsewhere*). Some mothers want their sons to move away and start better lives; others want their sons to remain close to home. All of them want their sons to turn out differently than their fathers did. Regardless of the details, Russo repeatedly portrays the exhausting, repetitive battles played out among families whose individual members are perpetually handicapped by qualities ranging from cruel selfishness to willed ignorance.

In the context of these turbulent family dynamics full of desperately unhappy marriages and lonely, often bewildered divorcees, it may seem remarkable that Richard Russo has been happily married to his wife, Barbara, since 1972. Almost all the marriages in Russo's fiction are, to paraphrase Tolstoy, unhappy in their own way. One common theme does seem to run through these miserable, divorced or soon-to-be-divorced couples: the deep disappointment that comes with failed expectations. Almost without exception, it is the women characters who are disappointed with their husbands. Anne leaves the irresponsible Dallas Younger in *Mohawk*; Jack Griffin nearly destroys his marriage in *That Old Cape Magic*; and in every novel in between we see evidence of husbands ill equipped to live up to their wives' relatively modest expectations. Not that Russo's world is devoid of unpleasant women; in *Nobody's Fool*, for example, Sully's ex-wife Vera is nearly impossible to live with (as even her current husband admits), and Rub's wife Bootsie is merely a caricature of every shrewish trait imaginable. In *Empire Falls*, Miles's ex-wife Janine is also painted as selfish and at times unkind, but Russo's portrayal of her is more multidimensional, and beyond her unsympathetic actions we see a woman who feels stifled by her small-town life and is desperate for a change—even when that change involves some regrettable decisions. For the most part, though, Russo's wives are patient and long-suffering, and he tends to portray them sympathetically. Before her ill-planned affair and subsequent nervous breakdown, Jenny Hall in *The Risk Pool* was a conscientious single mother who tried not to speak unkindly of her wayward and irresponsible estranged husband. In *Straight Man*, Hank Devereaux's wife patiently copes with her gleefully obnoxious husband. In *Bridge of Sighs*, Sarah Lynch is acutely aware of her husband's deliberately circumscribed life, and until the very end of the novel she stifles her criticism of Lou's excessive homebody tendencies. Joy, Jack Griffin's wife in *That Old Cape Magic*, endures Jack's maddening self-absorption and treats him with kindness, even while they are separated.

Critics have approached Russo's penchant for miserable marriages with a variety of reactions. Some see Russo as incapable or unwilling to portray a complicated female character and put her at the center of a novel. Indeed his women characters tend to take on exclusively supporting roles, and even those women clearly idolized by the main characters (Toby Roebuck in *Nobody's Fool*, Tria Ward in *The Risk Pool*) never come fully into focus. Another explanation is simply that those are not the stories Russo wishes to tell. The world he repeatedly returns to is a world of men. Women may serve drinks or even own the taverns, but the focus is largely on the men hunkered on the stools in front of the bars. *The Risk Pool*, although ostensibly Ned Hall's life story told from his point of view, is actually a story about the life of Sam Hall—a life of poker games, pool halls, fishing trips, construction jobs, and other activities that have little to do with women. His bonds are with his male friends, his drinking buddies, and, eventually, his son. Likewise, *Nobody's Fool* takes place primarily in environments where women may be present but do not dominate. Sully engages meaningfully with women in the novel, especially his landlord Beryl Peoples and his sometime girlfriend Ruth, but his deepest connections exist among his male friends and coworkers, with whom he feels liberated from the stifling expectations of disappointed women. In fact many of Russo's male characters find themselves constantly bewildered by women and their expectations, especially because they honestly believe they are doing the best they can.

Along with being characterized by critics as a "small-town" writer, Russo has justifiably been identified as one of America's finest contemporary comic writers. Amid scenes of heartbreak, unemployment, and life's disappointments, Russo perpetually finds the humorous angle that catapults the moment from melancholic to amusing. When asked in 2009 about his penchant for writing humor, he explained that he "discovered fairly early on that when the world isn't busy breaking our hearts, which it does on a daily, sometimes hourly basis, it's a damn entertaining place."[26] He also eschewed the notion that he is someone who "writes humor," instead claiming, "I'm simply reporting on the world I observe, which is frequently hilarious."[27] Russo's fiction encompasses the slapstick, as in *Straight Man*, when Professor Hank Devereaux creeps into the crawl space in the ceiling above the conference room in order to eavesdrop on a department meeting at which his professional future is being decided, or in *That Old Cape Magic*, when Jack Griffin's wheelchair-bound father-in-law lands wheels-up in a yew bush the night before his granddaughter's wedding. In addition it often includes examples of highly literate humor in its depiction of small, easily overlooked things that characters together find funny, as in Miles and Tick Roby's collection of ungrammatical signs in *Empire Falls* or Ned Hall and Claude Schwartz's identification of funny newspaper typos in *The Risk Pool*. But most often Russo's humor is delivered as a clever observation by the narrator, a deadpan turn of phrase that strikes to the heart of simultaneous realism and ludicrousness. Russo understands that comic writers are often dismissed as less substantial than other writers but does not let this attitude deter him. He acknowledged, "In 'serious' fiction . . . you can feel the weight of the material. You expect to see the effort and strain of all that heavy lifting, and we reward the effort as much as the success. Comedy is often just as serious, and to ignore that seriousness is misguided, of course, but most writers with comic world views have accustomed themselves to being sold at a discount. Most of us wouldn't have it any other way."[28]

Richard Russo's fiction, to date, has covered far more ground than perhaps he is given credit for. Resemblances appear across novels, to be sure, but his largely homogenous small towns yield a surprising diversity of perspectives, opinions, experiences, and attitudes among its residents. The tremendous impact of Russo's upbringing in Gloversville has left an indelible, undeniable mark on his fiction, even those stories not set in small, northeastern, blue-collar towns. Russo acknowledged his powerful connection to his hometown during a 2012 visit to Union College in Schenectady, located just an hour from Gloversville. "One of the great paradoxes of my life as a writer is that on the one hand I very seldom return to Gloversville anymore," he remarked, "whereas figuratively speaking I seldom leave it. Anyone looking for Gloversville in my novels starting with *Mohawk* in 1986 will have no trouble finding it. Gloversville and upstate New York run in my veins the way Dublin ran in Joyce's."[29]

CHAPTER 2

Mohawk

Richard Russo published his first novel, *Mohawk,* in 1986 while he was teaching in the English department at Southern Illinois University in Carbondale. Although he had already begun establishing himself as a talented writer, publishing stories such as "The Top of the Tree" (1981) in the *Mid-American Review,* "The Challenge Court" (1983) in *Sonora Review,* and "The Dowry" (1985) in *Prairie Schooner,* this first novel eluded him for a long time. Russo completed a five-hundred-page draft of it while still a graduate student at the University of Arizona, though in its early stages it barely resembled the *Mohawk* that was ultimately published. Set in Tucson, it focused on an embittered middle-aged woman named Anne Grouse. In an interview Russo described his difficulty trying to write about what he simply did not know. He explained, "The novel was floundering; the only parts of it that were alive at all were the flashbacks in Mohawk, the town [Anne] had left." A friend pointed this out to him, and Russo was forced to admit that "his comments made crushing sense. Of course, it involved throwing out everything except 75 pages, admitting that I'd written a bad book and going back and writing a better one."[1] In his revision Russo focused on people and places he understood intimately, from personal experience. He admitted to another interviewer that he "didn't know a damn thing about Tucson really. I was still a visitor there after ten years, but as soon as I went back to a place like the one I grew up in, I felt like I didn't have to do any research. I just kind of knew it."[2]

Going back to the places he knew meant revisiting Gloversville, and recasting it as the fictional world of Mohawk, New York. Like Gloversville, Mohawk was a failing tannery town full of unemployed or underemployed mill workers who lacked any sort of economic opportunity. Russo mined his hometown for countless details of the landscape he could use in his novel. The Nathan Littauer Hospital in Gloversville became the Nathan Littler Hospital in Mohawk; likewise the wealthy Kingsborough Road became a similarly affluent section in Mohawk called Kings Road. The Cayadutta Creek, which winds through Gloversville and was long tainted by runoff from the tanneries, became the poisoned Cayuga Creek in Mohawk (though there is a real Cayuga Creek in western New York state). Other down-and-out fictional towns that appear in Russo's novels, including North Bath, New York (in *Nobody's Fool*), Railton, Pennsylvania (in *Straight Man*), Empire Falls, Maine (in *Empire Falls*), and Thomaston, New York (in *Bridge of Sighs*), all resemble Gloversville to some extent; however, the town of Mohawk that features so prominently in *Mohawk* as well as in Russo's second novel, *The Risk Pool,* remains Russo's most thorough representation of his hometown.

Reviews of *Mohawk* were mixed, and its reception paled in comparison with his later, more polished, and ultimately more successful novels. *Kirkus Reviews* opened its brief discussion of *Mohawk* with the dismissive and derisive comment that it was a "Soapy first novel about life, love, passion, and perversion in a decaying mill-town in upstate New York" and ended with the lament that it left "not a cliché unturned."[3] Another critic noted that "the initially strong sympathy [Russo] evokes for his characters is gradually lost in the complex windings of plot and structure."[4] Other reviewers were somewhat more encouraging, although several did comment on what they saw as caricaturelike portrayals of some minor characters and the plot's overreliance on withheld secrets and implausible coincidences.[5] Nevertheless, Russo impressed at least a few critics with his sympathetic portrayal of hard-pressed workers struggling to build a future in a crumbling industrial town. The *New York Times*'s Michiko Kakutani in particular complimented Russo's ability "to convey to us [the characters'] essential decency and resilience in the face of loss—giving us an appreciation of their fortitude and wit, as well as their weaknesses and pain."[6]

In the nearly three decades since the appearance of *Mohawk,* Russo has published six additional novels, two collections of short stories, a memoir, and numerous other short pieces, both fiction and nonfiction. Given the range and depth of his subsequent output, the most important thing to recognize about *Mohawk* is that within it one finds the seeds of almost all his later works. This first novel reveals a writer deeply immersed in stories of socioeconomic class, the aspirations of upward mobility, the fears of downward mobility, and the tremendous challenges of just trying to maintain one's own hard-fought ground. Parent-child relationships break down in *Mohawk;* later novels such as *The Risk Pool, Nobody's Fool, Straight Man,* and *That Old Cape Magic* explore this theme with even greater depth, intensity, and poignancy. *Mohawk* introduces the painful toll that environmental contamination takes on the workers at manufacturing plants, a theme that Russo examines more closely in *Empire Falls* and *Bridge of Sighs.* In addition the despair engendered by the lack of opportunity in these bleak and circumscribed small towns haunts the lives of Mohawk's residents and, later, those of all Russo's other fictional towns. In short, *Mohawk* emerges as a solid, coherent, and moving novel in its own right, but the benefit of hindsight allows readers now to see it as an incubator for the themes that have come to characterize Russo's fiction.

Part 1 of *Mohawk* begins in 1967 in Mohawk, New York, a small upstate town whose once-thriving leather industry is now on the wane; part 2 takes place five years later, in 1972. The physical center of the story is the Mohawk Grill, a diner run by middle-aged Harry Saunders, a proprietor whose gruff exterior hides a compassionate heart and deep sympathy for and loyalty to the down-and-outers of Mohawk. The Mohawk Grill initiates a long series of modest eateries that anchor Russo's fiction: the Mohawk Grill features again in Russo's second novel, *The Risk Pool;* the Empire Grill serves a similar function in *Empire Falls,* as does Hattie's diner in *Nobody's Fool* and Ikey's corner store in *Bridge of Sighs.*

Harry runs a relatively successful business, especially given the boarded-up tanneries and the high unemployment that plague Mohawk. He protects his customers from the overeager ticketing of the police officer Walter Gaffney and offers kindness and the occasional free breakfast to "Wild Bill" Gaffney, the thirty-something handicapped man who is casually mistreated by many of the adults and children he encounters in Mohawk. Harry quickly emerges as a pillar of moral responsibility in the novel; his attention to detail may not be good (his wall calendars are usually a year off), but his moral compass, sorely tested through the course of the novel, is dead on.

Mohawk chronicles the stories of two Mohawk families, the Grouses and the Gaffneys, whose lives intersect over the course of three generations; the novel's sixty-seven short chapters depict, nonlinearly and often obliquely, the complicated relationships among the primary dozen or so characters. The Grouse family is led by its patriarch, Mather Grouse, who tries to exert control over his wife, their adult daughter, Anne; Anne's ex-husband, Dallas; and Anne's son, Randall. The Gaffney family is headed by Rory Gaffney, whose tense and mysterious relationship with Mather Grouse provides the foundation for much of the suspense in the story. Rory's mentally disabled son, Bill; Rory's younger brother, Walter; and Rory's granddaughter, B. G.; also slalom in and out of the lives of the Grouse family.

The *New York Times* critic Michiko Kakutani noted that the characters in *Mohawk* lead "not terribly eventful lives," but although their day-to-day worlds may seem relatively mundane, the novel is punctuated by multiple events of life-changing proportion. A car accident permanently paralyzes Dan Wood, who continues to pine after Anne Grouse even after he marries Anne's cousin. A devastating fire destroys the town's hospital and makes a hero out of young Randall Younger, who inadvertently saves the life of Bill Gaffney, a man irreparably brain damaged by a savage beating administered by his father. Diana Wood, Dan's wife, dies young and unexpectedly. Dallas Younger's brother also dies young, of cancer, and Dallas's niece is thought to suffer from leukemia. A brutal fistfight between Randall and several other high school boys results in a serious hospitalization for one teenager. Incest poisons the life of Randall's girlfriend B. G. The police officer Walt Gaffney brutally murders his brother, Rory, and his nephew, Bill, before turning his pistol on himself. The Vietnam War draft-dodging Randall, who is wrong-fully arrested for Rory's murder, avoids prosecution when the case against him falls apart; he subsequently manages to evade two Selective Service agents by escaping out a courthouse window and disappearing from town. Amid all this drama flows the placid and seemingly unchanging world of Mohawk, a town of underemployed blue-collar workers who hold out little hope for advancement or opportunity.

Since the publication of *Mohawk,* readers and critics alike have noted Richard Russo's ability to evoke a profound sense of place in his fiction. His depictions of life in small towns, particularly small towns each with more of a past than a future, have been lauded for their sympathetic details and for capturing the authentic rhythms of life. In interviews, however, Russo has repeatedly emphasized his focus on socioeconomic class rather than the specifics of a particular location. In *Mohawk* the importance of class and related economic opportunity (or its absence) surfaces not only in the stories of the laid-off tannery workers who hang around the Mohawk Grill and the Off Track Betting (OTB) parlor but also in Anne Grouse's struggles to find work for which she is suited and in Randall's recognition that his hometown offers him nothing in the way of a successful future. Class issues are also embedded in the physical nature of the town itself, as Russo clearly establishes the literal boundaries that separate members of different socioeconomic classes. In Mohawk wealthy residents live on Kings Road (in a bit of heavy-handed symbolism), "a dead-end street whose residents' lives were punctuated by worries no more serious than the occasional slice or duck-hook" (16). Of course this proves to be not entirely true, as Dan and Diana Wood, residents of Kings Road, suffer serious worries about their marriage, their finances, Dan's physical and mental health, and the role of Diana's domineering and demanding mother, Milly, in their lives. Nevertheless, Russo makes it clear that the people with the big houses and swimming pools along Kings Road experience life in Mohawk very differently than do the townspeople who live in the more modest neighborhoods, such as the Grouses, or in the shabby houses and trailers on the outskirts of town, such as the Gaffneys. His focus in *Mohawk*, as it proves to be in all his other small-town novels, is on the folks who live in the run-down houses, whose roofs leak and whose rents are overdue. The people living on the very edge of solvency, who are one tough break away from losing it all, are the ones Russo portrays most vividly, with compassion and humor and, above all, understanding.

In *Mohawk*, Russo sets the stories of the Grouses and the Gaffneys, as well as the other working-class characters, against the alarmingly toxic background of widespread environmental contamination by the Mohawk tanneries. The industrial poisoning and toxic waste that figure prominently in *Mohawk* initiate a thematic pattern that reappears in several other Russo novels; for example in *Empire Falls* the trash and pollutants in the Knox River inspire C. B. Whiting to engineer a change in the river's path, and in *Bridge of Sighs* the Cayoga Stream, which runs through Thomaston, is poisoned by run-off dyes from local tanneries. Indeed, Russo's own childhood in Gloversville, New York, a small town historically rooted in a once-flourishing leather industry, provided the author with many firsthand details about unnatural colors and odors emanating from local waterways.

Russo's portrayal of Mohawk's toxic tanneries begins in the first chapter and reveals not only the extent of the poisonings but also the local residents' almost wholehearted disinterest in the situation, which would be comic if it were not also so tragic. Harry Saunders picks up a copy of the *Mohawk Republican*, whose front-page headline reads "Tanneries Blamed for Abnormal Area Cancer Rate." The story reports that Mohawk County residents are "three times more likely to contract cancer, leukemia, and several other serious diseases than elsewhere in the country. Persons who work in the tanneries and leather mills themselves or who reside near the Cayuga Creek, where the Morelock, Hunter, and Cayuga tanneries are accused of dumping, are ten to twenty times more likely to contract one of the diseases listed on page B-6." But Russo leaves the final punch for the end. The article concludes, "Spokesmen for the tanneries deny that any dumping has occurred in nearly two decades and suggest that the recent findings are in all probability a statistical anomaly" (6). The tragicomic last line of the article clearly dismisses the findings of this report, but the inclusion of this news so early in the novel serves to establish the citizens of Mohawk as victims of, and in some cases unwitting accomplices in, the destruction of their own health. Yet this so-called news does not appear to surprise any of Mohawk's citizens; Harry leaves the paper on the counter of the Mohawk Grill so customers can check the racing results or the lucky number. There is no sense that the story about alarmingly high cancer rates will have much impact on the lives of these citizens.

Nevertheless environmental contamination does not disappear with yesterday's newspaper. This element of tainted life in Mohawk repeatedly surfaces in various contexts, even those unrelated to the lives of actual tannery workers. For example, when Anne Grouse waits for her cousin Diana to arrive at a Holiday Inn, Anne looks out the window at the Cayuga Creek and the narrator explains, "Her father said there were trout in the stream when he came to Mohawk as a young man. But the fish began to come out looking bulbous, and the Fish-and-Game quit stocking it. Recently there was talk of restocking, and to show that the past was past the tanneries were in favor of it" (83). This detail never surfaces in actual conversations between the characters, but its presence, via indirect discourse, emphasizes the relentless portrayal of the natural world as corrupted, threatening, and perhaps irreversibly damaged. The implicit question remains for readers: If the fish could be so horribly mutated, what of the people?

Indeed the town collectively and casually acknowledges the implications of the poisoned creek during the search for Will Bill Gaffney, who disappeared after rescuing Randall Younger from a beating by one of his classmates, and in the process badly injured another boy by tossing him against a dumpster. Some of the callers contacting police with alleged tips about Gaffney's whereabouts "were Wild Bill's classmates many years ago, and they remembered him, now that they stopped to think, as never having been exactly right. For years he had been drinking the contaminated water of the Cayuga Creek, which had given him brain cancer. The whole town was on the lookout, conventional wisdom being that a man with a brain half-eaten away with contamination couldn't outsmart the constabulary and citizenry of Mohawk County for more than a few days" (128). The understated humor of the last line contrasts with the steady and sinister background that the poisoned stream, and by implication the tanneries, provides the story.

The townspeople's matter-of-fact acceptance of the notion that drinking from the Cayuga Creek naturally caused brain cancer might suggest widespread belief in the tanneries' responsibilities for compromising the health of

Mohawk residents, but this does not appear to be the case. When the elderly Mr. Anadio, one of Mather Grouse's former coworkers at the tannery, recognizes Mather in Greenie's Tavern, he tearfully announces to Mather that he is dying of cancer. He says, "'They killed us, Mather. All them years. . . . Killed us, but they won't admit it.' Tears were welling up in his eyes. 'They wouldn't admit it if it was a thousand times the average. A million. Not them bastards'" (199). Remarkably this argument never seems to gain much traction among the former tannery employees despite its apparent truth. When Rory Gaffney steps in to defend the tanneries as the only places where men such as themselves could earn their livings, the issue of environmental contamination once again recedes, at least temporarily. The repeated references to the poisoned Cayuga Creek, however, effectively move this background element to the foreground, and as a result the novel becomes deeply engaged in the tanneries' egregious betrayal of Mohawk's citizens.

The notion of a literally poisonous environment pervades not just *Mohawk* but several of Russo's other novels as well. The perpetrators are inevitably local manufacturing plants that employ townspeople in good times and lay them off, sometimes seasonally and sometimes permanently, in bad times, all the while dumping tons of toxic waste into area waterways. But the bitterness one might expect from those victimized and, sometimes, sickened by the pollution is far from uniform. Mr. Anadio feels betrayed by the tanneries that, he believes, caused his cancer, but Rory Gaffney acknowledges that these same tanneries kept the town economically viable. Similarly the narrator in "Poison," a short story collected in *The Whore's Child*, recalls that in his hometown, "chemical byproducts were dumped into the river until the water tasted like brass and the fish grew tumors the size of golf balls" (160). Yet the narrator's dying father, "who grew one of those golf balls in his brain," asks his son, without irony, "where would a man like me have been without that mill?" (165). In nearly all of his so-called blue-collar fiction, Russo maintains a consistent tension between the destruction that mills and tanneries wreak on the economic and physical health of the workers and the loyalty that the workers feel for the industries that poison their water and yet at the same time provide them with the paychecks to feed their families.

The townspeople's loyalty to the destructive force of the tanneries does not, however, prevent them from acknowledging the corruption that, for some, defines the experience of working at such plants. When Harry Saunders scolds Officer Gaffney for chasing after the missing Wild Bill Gaffney instead of fighting more serious crimes, he says, "I can tell you about who's stealing leather over to the Tucker Tannery, and who's cutting and selling it, too. Unless maybe you already know. And then you can go after Old Man Tucker himself and jail his ass for all that shit in the crick that's making the whole county sick" (149). Harry not only acknowledges the crime of toxic pollution in the water but also implies that both men know that Officer Gaffney's brother, Rory, is stealing and selling leather from one of the tanneries. Rory Gaffney, we learn, has been stealing skins with impunity for a long time. Years before, when Mather Grouse was promoted to foreman at the tannery, Rory had approached him in the bathroom. The narrator relays the encounter, via indirect discourse: "Nothing would be required of him. He [Mather] would simply look the other way. Skins were always disappearing, and had been disappearing for so long that if they stopped disappearing it would be noticed and then a lot of people would be in trouble. Besides, the owners were the biggest crooks of all, only for them it was all legit. That's the way it was in America" (203). Mather rejected the plan to collude in this illegal scheme and shortly afterward gave up his promotion and returned to his former position, from which he was soon laid off. Russo allows us no sentimental notion of ethical behavior being rewarded; in *Mohawk*, it seems, nobody prospers by following the rules. Long after Gaffney had retired from the tannery, he persisted in stealing skins. In part 2 he even involves Randall Younger in his scheme to transport stolen skins out of town, reveling in the irony that Mather's grandson proves willing to do what the incorruptible Mather would not.

This tension that emerges from a sense of loyalty to a destructive force appears not just in the context of industrial labor. Indeed this tension helps define numerous complicated and often fractured parent-child relationships. Russo's fiction is peppered with parents and children who struggle to communicate and who frequently lack empathy or understanding for the other. Russo returns to this troubled parent-child dynamic in *The Risk Pool, Nobody's Fool, Straight Man, That Old Cape Magic,* and in some of his short fiction as well; *Mohawk* is particularly infused with parent-child relationships that are essentially unsatisfying to either party. Sometimes communication lines never develop, as in the case of Dallas Younger and his son Randall, or they are irreparably damaged over time, as with Mather Grouse and his daughter Anne. Notions of responsibility and guilt replace love and affection; children drift away from parents, and neither has any idea how to reconnect.

Perhaps the most central parent-child relationship in the novel belongs to Mather Grouse and his daughter Anne. Although they clearly care for one another, their relationship lacks warmth and affection, and Mather "wanted many times to tell her how much he missed the closeness they had shared when she was a girl. He knew he was to blame, but knowing and knowing what to do about it were two different things" (154). Mather's feelings for Anne are complicated, for she has disappointed him in the one true goal he set for her: to leave Mohawk and seek a better life elsewhere (this theme of parents trying to motivate their children to leave their stagnant hometowns also reemerges in several later Russo novels). "Long after he had quietly surrendered his personal dream," Russo writes, "Mather Grouse continued to dream for his daughter. At the risk of turning her into a snob, he began to suggest to Anne that there was more to life than Mohawk had to offer" (206). Mather also feels guilty for an incestuous dream he had about Anne when she was still the prettiest girl in high school (although the incest theme goes no further within the Grouse household, it does reappear in the shocking sexual relationship that Rory Gaffney has with his granddaughter). Mather and Anne struggle to talk honestly, but in the end they remain deeply disconnected from each other's lives. Later, well after Mather Grouse has died, Anne finds it difficult to reconcile her feelings for her father. She ultimately admits to herself that she neither hates nor adores her father (348) but rather feels disappointed in herself that she had "canonized" her father and, as a result, misinterpreted and misunderstood him. She realizes, too late, that she "had always been aware of his fear, rage, anguish, and disappointment, though she hadn't allowed him these because she had counted on him to rescue her from her own" (349).

Anne's feelings toward her mother are not much more generous than those toward her father. As an elderly widow, Mrs. Grouse clings to Anne and, to a lesser extent, Randall, and at the same time she tries, fairly successfully, to manipulate them into acquiescing to her every wish. When Mather dies, she convinces Anne and Randall, on the verge of moving to Connecticut, to abandon their plans and stay with her in Mohawk. Anne feels obligated to help her mother but appears to feel no particular warmth toward her. Neither does Anne seem especially connected to her son, whom she barely recognizes when he reappears in the second part of the novel after time away at college and about whose final disappearance she makes no comment. She refers to him once, aloofly, as a "strange boy" (214) after he risks his life to save Wild Bill Gaffney from the hospital fire. Anne's complicated relationships with her parents and with her son foreshadow dozens of future families chronicled in Russo's fiction whose members struggle to understand and to express their feelings for one another.

Russo's fiction often illuminates those human experiences where feelings of desperation and hopefulness merge in the lives of struggling small-town residents. The despair that workers feel when laid off for the season, for instance, blends with their hope that they will be lucky enough to be called back when the shop doors reopen. The struggles to find true love blend with the hope of becoming one who is truly loved. The discouragement of constant financial stress fuses with the inveterate optimism that comes from playing a lucky number or betting on a hot jockey. Indeed gambling is the hobby of choice for the unemployed and disfranchised in Mohawk, a theme that resurfaces in *The Risk Pool, Nobody's Fool,* and, to a lesser extent, *Empire Falls* and *Bridge of Sighs.* In *Mohawk* the OTB, the racetrack, and various poker games provide Randall Younger and his crowd with ample outlets for gambling, but the most important figure within this small-town gaming circle is undoubtedly Untemeyer, the "workingman's bookie who took no heavy action, but no wager was too small and for this reason he was a favorite among men who often lacked the traditional two-dollar bet" (190). In *Mohawk* we have the first example of an unexpected lottery winner (*Nobody's Fool* has the second), when Mather Grouse plays the daily number exactly one time, on the day before his death. His ten-dollar bet—a large sum for the small-time bookie—yields an impressive return, but when Untemeyer appears at the Grouse home just after Mather's funeral to attempt to deliver the payout, Anne and Mrs. Grouse confusedly turn him away. Mrs. Grouse's certainty that Mather "was no common gambler" (229) causes her to reject the payout, and the upsetting encounter with Untemeyer leads her to demand that Anne and Randall cancel their plans to relocate to Connecticut and instead stay in Mohawk with her. Mather certainly could not have anticipated that his onetime bet would result in sealing off his daughter's exit from Mohawk, a path that he had for years encouraged her to follow.

Gambling surfaces in other ways in *Mohawk,* particularly in Dallas Younger's life. For example when Dallas is eighteen, he takes Anne to the racetrack at Saratoga for opening day. Their experience at Saratoga exemplifies Russo's portrayal of the differences between Mohawk and the "outside world" and how residents sometimes react to their encounters with other environments. It quickly becomes apparent to Anne that Dallas's clothes and manners do not come close to meeting the standards of the lovely old hotel where they dined or even the racetrack full of wealthy and refined horse enthusiasts. Dallas bets foolishly on the races that day and loses all his money, and his disappointment in the entire experience is tempered only by the deep sense of relief he feels at returning home that evening, where he knows how to fit in (94–96). (Incidentally this pattern of a young man leaving his hometown briefly, having an uncomfortable or unpleasant experience, and then returning home full of gratefulness and relief surfaces in several other Russo novels. Jimmy Minty in *Empire Falls* has a similar experience when he visits a college campus, and Lucy Lynch can hardly wait to return to Thomaston after a stint at college.) A lousy day at Saratoga does not prevent Dallas from continuing to gamble but instead merely teaches him that he is better off gambling close to home, where everything makes more sense to him.

The presence of the OTB and local bookies in the culture of Mohawk serves to deepen Russo's portrayal of a town shattered by economic instability. With a significant portion of the population out of work or underemployed, men have both the motivation to try to "hit it big" and the time to spend studying racing forms at the Empire Grill and hanging around at the OTB. Russo portrays these men not as especially shiftless, and certainly not as amoral, but rather as merely aimless and, despite the odds, still hopeful that today would be the day they would get their big break. Gambling provides them with a social network, a reliable subculture of men like themselves, perhaps beaten down but still looking for that windfall that will bring something better. As the narrator explains of the early-morning customers at the Empire Grill, each armed with racing forms, "there are many systems for picking winners at the track, and each of the regulars . . . has his own, though as they readily admit no system's perfect or the players would all live in Florida" (414). The gamblers remain undeterred, though, by consistent failure, and they understand implicitly that "poring over the charts of workout times and track conditions, analyzing the level of competition—these are pleasurable activities in themselves" (414). The pleasure associated with gambling is, in some capacity, actually divorced from the goal of winning, for as the narrator notes, "the afficionados [sic] were the first to admit you can't beat the horses. Or the dice. Or the cards. All you can do is try" (415).

Mohawk is a novel full of characters whose dreams, which are far from extravagant, never seen to come true. The characters yearn for meaningful relationships, steady work, and some security in their lives, and yet even these modest hopes seem too much to ask. Nevertheless, despite the melancholic tone that inevitably accompanies such disappointments, Russo manages to write what at times is a very funny novel. His gift for portraying comedic dialogue or for skewering a character with a deft and witty comment provides the leavening that this otherwise grim novel desperately needs. The absurdly intense and competitive relationship between Mrs. Grouse and her older sister, Milly, for example, is rendered with great wit. The two elderly women revel in their respective miseries, both physical and emotional, and after Mather Grouse dies, the narrator explains that up until this point, "burying her husband had given Milly something of an unfair advantage over Mrs. Grouse since both women derived great satisfaction from loading onto their slender shoulders every hardship life could impose. If anything,

Mrs. Grouse now had the upper hand, having both a deceased husband and a divorced daughter to her credit. But she was too kind to press an unfair advantage, and the two agreed that each had leaden crosses to bear" (249). Mrs. Grouse's burden is magnified further by her terror at the idea of worms living in her front yard. Although she never actually witnesses a worm, she notices that the lawn is covered with holes that the neighbor tells her are made by night crawlers that come up after the rain. Mrs. Grouse's subsequent obsession with, and war on, the harmless and, frankly, invisible worms provides another point of comic absurdity while at the same time demonstrating the power that an irrational fear can exert.

As *Mohawk* was a debut novel with many significant strengths, it is impossible to read it alongside Russo's later works and not see the extent to which the author has developed and matured as a storyteller. Despite *Mohawk*'s sometimes dizzying nonlinearity, Russo attempts in the book what he achieves in later novels: the use of disfranchised, white, small-town, blue-collar workers as the lens through which to view much larger social and human issues of love, loss, and opportunity. Russo's talent for third-person omniscient narration surfaces in *Mohawk*, as does his burgeoning ability to tell stories with unusually large casts of characters. These techniques are developed more fully in his subsequent novels, particularly *Empire Falls* and *Bridge of Sighs*.

At the conclusion of *Mohawk*, Russo neatly ties up every loose end. Although the lives of the characters are forever altered by the events chronicled in the novel, none of their futures remains particularly mysterious to readers. The Gaffney men have all been killed. Dan, now a widower, decides to build a new life with Anne in Arizona (the state, incidentally, to which Russo fled when the opportunity arose to leave Gloversville and attend college). The elderly Mrs. Grouse and her sister Milly, are comfortably lodged in an apartment of their own, with nobody to bother but each other. Dallas seems destined to find a future with Loraine, his brother's widow. Randall remains a draft dodger on the lam from the Selective Service, but he "liked the fact that his was a sizable country, large enough to stay lost in without exactly running away" (351). Even B. G., Randall's erstwhile girlfriend, seems more or less satisfied about reconciling with her husband Andy now that he is out of prison. The novel returns in its closing moments to where it began: behind the counter of the Mohawk Grill, with Harry Saunders frying sausage and talking horses with the workingmen who, in Russo's imagination, define the town of Mohawk.

CHAPTER 3

The Risk Pool

Richard Russo's second novel, *The Risk Pool* (1988), returns to the fictional town of Mohawk, New York, the setting of his first novel, a generation before the story told in *Mohawk*. *The Risk Pool* begins around the time of World War II and extends into the early 1980s. A number of characters and many settings featured in *Mohawk* reappear in this second novel, including the Mohawk Grill, its proprietor Harry Saunders, Greenie's Tavern, Our Lady of Sorrows Catholic Church, Untemeyer the bookie, Wild Bill Gaffney, and several other place, street, and family names. More important than the repeated physical and human landscapes, though, several themes first addressed in *Mohawk* are revisited in *The Risk Pool* and begin to establish patterns in Russo's fiction that will extend throughout much of his published work. *The Risk Pool* reprises the issue of environmental contamination that surfaced in *Mohawk,* specifically the tanneries' culpability in poisoning the water and the people of Mohawk. It also addresses the financial despair that accompanies life within a marginal economy that barely sustains itself, let alone offers future opportunities. But the two most significant themes that Russo tackles in *The Risk Pool* are dysfunctional and unstable families, especially their effects on children who find themselves in unpredictable situations, and the ongoing issues of socioeconomic inequality, specifically how the have-nots find ways to live in the same world as the haves.

Overall, critics received *The Risk Pool* with admiration, noting, in several cases, the improvement in Russo's narrative craftsmanship from that of his previous novel. Reviewers such as Michiko Kakutani, who praised *Mohawk* in the pages of the *New York Times,* admitted that *The Risk Pool* clearly outstrips its predecessor in narrative grace: "[Russo's] previous novel's tendency to veer precipitately into melodrama has been chastened here (the violent events that do occur simply seem a part of contemporary life's uncertainty), and its twisting plot, so reliant on portentously withheld secrets, has been replaced by a straightforward and newly authoritative narrative."[1] The *New York Times Book Review* echoed this opinion that Russo's writing had matured, noting, "Even more than in 'Mohawk,' with its busier plot and leaner texture, Mr. Russo proves himself a master at evoking the sights, feelings and especially smells of a town in a tailspin."[2] The *Library Journal* added its own praise for *The Risk Pool,* commenting that the novel "is filled with wonderfully drawn characters and hilarious adventures but the subtext is one of sadness and near desperation."[3] Almost without exception, reviewers complimented Russo's talent for portraying the rhythms and details of small-town life and painting a tragicomic portrait of the lives of ordinary people in a dead-end town.

The Risk Pool opens with an epigraph borrowed from the opening paragraph of John Steinbeck's *Cannery Row* (1945), which suggests Russo's deliberate effort to portray his down-and-out characters on their own terms, without judgment and certainly without condemnation. The epigraph reads, "Its inhabitants are, as the man once said, 'whores, pimps, gamblers, and sons of bitches,' by which he meant Everybody. Had the man looked through another peephole he might have said, 'Saints, and angels and martyrs and holy men,' and he would have meant the same thing." The epigraph refers to the residents and workers of the area in Monterey, California, where the fish canneries operated, but in Russo's vision it could apply to the inhabitants of any working-class community. Russo has acknowledged his admiration for Steinbeck and particularly for *Cannery Row* for its masterful omniscient narration, and this passage suggests too the power of the omniscient narrator to dictate readers' responses to the scene played out in front of them.

The Risk Pool is dedicated to Jim Russo, the author's father, who suffered from cancer during much of the time the novel was being written and died before it was completed. Richard Russo has commented in interviews that *The Risk Pool* is an especially personal novel for him, one in which he tried to work out many of the complex emotions he felt toward his father, and many parallels exist between Sam Hall and Jimmy Russo. Like Sam Hall, Jimmy Russo served in World War II, landing on Utah Beach on D-day and fighting from the French shore all the way to Germany. But after winning a Bronze Star and returning to Gloversville, he could never manage to settle down into the standard routine of family life. Instead of mill work, he found a place working on road construction crews, and he soon abandoned his wife and infant son for a life of bars, pool, and poker games. He never left Gloversville for long, however, and the young Russo encountered his father from time to time around town; during the summers while he was in college, he even worked alongside his father on such road crews (as Ned Hall does in the novel). Other episodes too in *The Risk Pool* echo Russo's real life; Russo's mother, Jean, worked for a time as a telephone operator, as Jenny Hall does in the novel, and Richard Russo served as an altar boy, as does Ned Hall. Despite the many parallels between Russo's life and his characters' lives in the novel, though, *The Risk Pool* is far from strictly autobiographical. Russo explained in a 1988 interview, "The deepest feelings of *The Risk Pool* are traceable to me and my father. . . . On the other hand, I never lived with him. All the major episodes are wholly imaginary."⁴ Still, readers can glean a reasonably accurate picture of some elements of life in 1950s Gloversville, during the years of Russo's childhood, through the adventures of Ned Hall as a child in Mohawk.

The Risk Pool's narrator is the often baffled but genuinely likable Ned Hall, and the story he tells begins before he was born and extends well into his adult life, as he struggles to understand what kind of man he has become and to what extent his father has influenced this development. Unlike *Mohawk*, which relies on an omniscient narrator, *The Risk Pool* engages a first-person narrative style that expands to a more general omniscience, at times, to include details about things that Ned could not possibly have known firsthand (such as the scenes that took place before he was born) and even thoughts belonging to other characters (particularly those of his father). The story is told primarily in the past tense, from the perspective of a mature adult looking back on his childhood and, later, his early adulthood. Although the story ends when the narrator is about thirty-five years old and seeing his newborn son for the first time, even this final chapter is told in the past tense, making the precise age of the narrator uncertain. A few clues in the text, however, suggest that the present-day narrator is just a little older than Ned Hall at the end of the novel; one such indication appears during a frustrating episode the twelve-year-old Ned experiences with his father and Drew Littler that, in the telling, prompts the narrator to note with surprise, "I was full of hatred so black that I can still taste it now, almost twenty-five years later" (141). These occasional narrative asides, written in the present tense, suggest that the mature narrator is still very much in the process of working out the meaning of his story even as he tells it. In these moments the narrator deliberately intrudes on his own tale in order to muse on the experience of revisiting episodes in his life from across the distance of several decades. In another such example, the narrator self-consciously admits to his readers, using present tense, "Now, so many years after the fact, it is possible for me to see the dark comedy of these events, but at the time I saw nothing amusing about [them]" (246–47). These intermittent shifts in perspective add a deeply nostalgic quality to the narrative, not so much by idealizing the story of Ned's childhood, which is neither idealized nor ideal, but rather by reminding the reader of the narrative distance between the teller and the tale and in the process presenting this story of life in Mohawk as both a bildungsroman and a glimpse of a lost world.

The novel is composed of four parts that correspond to the four seasons of the year in Mohawk, as cynically described by Ned Hall's late grandfather: "Fourth of July," "Mohawk Fair," "Eat the Bird," and "Winter." The first part, "Fourth of July," begins just after World War II and shortly before Ned's birth to Jenny Hall, a hardworking mother who longs for warmer climes, and Sam Hall, a father who cannot begin to comply with or even understand the constraints that accompany family life. The story skips ahead quickly to 1953, when young Ned is a first-grader and explains his father's absence from their home by telling his schoolmates that his father is dead. Sam promptly appears at Ned's elementary school to confront him about this lie, and for much of the rest of Ned's early childhood the tension between absent and present father accelerates. Sam drifts in and out of Ned's life. At one point he kidnaps Ned overnight to take him fishing; a close version of this section of the novel was published separately as a short story called "Fishing with Wussy" in 1986 in the British journal *Granta*. Sam is portrayed as the ultimate reckless—even dangerous—father, and yet the narrative slips into a third-person retrospective mode to reveal that Sam never thought of himself as dangerous and cannot imagine how or why his wife has come to think so (34). The discrepancy between how others see Sam and how he sees himself continues throughout the novel.

Later in the first section of *The Risk Pool*, Ned's mother becomes so emotionally incapacitated by her brief romantic liaison with a young Catholic priest that she can no longer work or even leave the house, and she becomes deeply dependent on antianxiety prescription drugs. After two years of this increasingly isolated life, Ned again encounters his father, whom he has not seen since the fishing trip five years before, and Sam invites the now twelve-year-old boy to come live with him "for a while" (88). The story then follows Ned as he tries to adjust to living with his father, who lacks all traditional parenting skills and largely leaves the boy to fend for himself. At the end of this section, Ned's mother suffers a complete nervous breakdown and is temporarily institutionalized, an event that inspires Ned to break into Klein's Department Store and steal as much as he could carry, an act of "pure malice" (127) that allows him to channel his pent-up rage at his mother into a new outlet.

The second section of the novel, "Mohawk Fair," follows the next two years of Ned's life, from ages twelve to fourteen, as it intersects with the lives of his father, his father's girlfriend Eileen Littler, and Eileen's teenage son, Drew, an angry and destructive boy. Ned learns to live among the men of Mohawk, eating alongside them in the Mohawk Diner and spending time in the bars and pool halls of the town. He cultivates his obsession with the wealthy Ward family, especially the beautiful daughter Tria Ward, and accumulates a tidy savings account by washing dishes at the Mohawk Diner, cleaning the beauty salon across from his father's apartment, and operating a successful, if illicit, used golf ball business. By the end of the section, though, as the increasingly unstable Drew Littler seems ready to destroy himself with rage and bitterness, Ned's mother returns from the rehabilitation center and promptly takes her son home with her. Sam Hall then disappears from town, and the voice of Ned's adult self says, "I didn't see him again for ten years" (268).

Part 3, "Eat the Bird," picks up Ned's story ten years later, around 1971, when he is about twenty-four years old and languishing in a cultural anthropology graduate program in Tucson, Arizona. Unfulfilled by his studies and developing a serious gambling problem, Ned has already decided to leave graduate school when he receives a call from Eileen Littler telling him that his alcoholic father needs someone to help look after him. Ned leaves for Mohawk almost immediately, and upon returning to his hometown he finds himself quickly caught up in the rhythms of his father's peripatetic life. Ned justifies his appearance in Mohawk in the middle of the semester by explaining that he has decided to conduct research for his thesis on "social hierarchy among primitive societies" (310), a ludicrous tale that his lithium-addled mother accepts unquestioningly. Ned immediately finds work as a bartender and begins drinking and socializing with Sam and his friends on a regular basis. He also dates Tria Ward briefly and edits for publication her grandfather's nearly impenetrable tome, *The History of Mohawk County*, at the request of Tria's mother. The section ends with Ned's mother and her new husband, lawyer F. William Peterson, moving to California; Ned's departure for New York City; and Drew Littler's gruesome and nearly inevitable death in a motorcycle accident.

The fourth and final section of *The Risk Pool*, "Winter," is the shortest of the novel and skips ahead in time about ten years, to Ned's mid-thirties and his new life as an editor in New York City and relatively estranged from both his parents. Sam initiates their reconnection after learning that he has cancer, and the final chapters of the novel are devoted to the relationship that Ned and Sam manage to resurrect in the months leading up to Sam's death. The epilogue encompasses Sam's death, the extraordinary and wildly alcoholic "send off" that Mohawk throws in Sam's honor, and, finally, the birth of Ned's son, described using much of the same language used to depict Ned's birth at the beginning of the novel. Thus, Russo ends *The Risk Pool* on a cyclical note, posing readers with the question of whether and to what extent Sam's history of erratic, if well-meaning, behavior will manifest itself in Ned's and his son's lives.

The Risk Pool encompasses a number of themes that have become characteristic of Russo's work. The first is the relationship between parents and children, and in this novel Russo executes a clever, if sometimes sad, reversal of the typical parent-child dynamic. From a young age Ned begins to adopt a protective, parental relationship toward his mother. At first his role as protector is minor and perhaps not unusual; for example, he chooses to keep from her information about certain incidents that he knows would upset her, as when his father appeared on their porch one day, indirectly encouraged Ned to climb higher into the tree than he had ever dared before, and then asked the six-year-old, "You figure you can keep a secret?" before disappearing through the neighborhood (17–18). Then just a week later, after his father kidnapped and then returned Ned after taking him on an overnight fishing trip, Ned never reveals to his mother the details of those two days with his father, sparing her the pain of hearing about the various dangers he had encountered.

Sam disappears for about five years after the fishing trip, during which time Ned and Jenny carry on a reasonably normal life, but during the summer when Ned is eleven years old, Jenny indulges in a brief affair with the young priest of the parish, Father Michaels, who has functioned effectively as a surrogate father for Ned. The priest, traumatized by their sin, abandons the church during mass the following Sunday; Jenny, perhaps more traumatized by Father Michaels's desertion than the affair, sinks deeper and deeper into serious depression. Over the next two years Ned takes on the role of caretaker for his invalid mother, who quits her job and eventually refuses to leave her house. Finally, his father's unlikely invitation for Ned to come live with him "for a while" (88) seems the best option available to Ned. He commences visiting his mother on Saturdays, to help her with her banking and to try to cheer her up, but it quickly becomes clear to him that she cannot tolerate any mention of Sam Hall. So Ned responds by inventing stories to tell her. "Rigid slavishness to the truth had never been one of my particular vices," the adult narrator explains, "and it was during this period that my mother's and my relationship was entirely rewritten, grounded firmly in kind falsehoods. It would never change again. For the rest of our lives I would lie and she would believe me" (116). Ned adopts a double life of sorts, conveying his many imagined successes (excellent grades, social success) to his mother, even as his actual school performance worsens and he engages in weekly shoplifting excursions in the department store below his father's apartment (117). In the absence of anyone else to look after his mother, Ned accepts, without really questioning it, the position as her protector, a parental role that lasts well into Ned's adulthood (and partially mirrors Russo's own relationship with his mother).

Although young Ned finds himself parenting, to a certain extent, his own mother, no true parental figure exists for Ned. His relationship with his father certainly deepens after they begin sharing an apartment, and they find common ground in the games they play together, especially billiards. But Ned is basically left to shift for himself; Sam is frequently absent, and so Ned eats on credit at the Mohawk Grill when he gets hungry and amuses himself playing pool and riding his bike around town. Although Ned's nuclear family is shattered, Russo portrays a different kind of family developing to fill the void. "Lest it seem that I was neglected," the narrator comments about his twelve-year-old self, "I should point out that once I became known to the Mohawk Grill crowd, it was like having about two dozen more or less negligent fathers whose slender attentions and vague goodwill nevertheless added up" (119). Despite the "slender attentions" of these down-and-outers, Ned is without question the most neglected child in all of Russo's fiction; bad parents abound in his novels, but with the exception of Ned, the children always have at least one parent looking after their basic needs. In Ned, Russo explores what can happen to a bright, kind young boy who, through no malice on his parents' part, is faced with the challenge of basically raising himself.

Eventually this experiment in self-raising comes to an end; Jenny Hall leaves the sanitarium addicted to lithium but otherwise capable of managing her household and resuming care of her son. Only after returning to his mother's home as a fourteen-year-old does Ned begin to interpret those two years with his father, in hindsight, as ones of fairly complete degeneracy. As Ned's older self recalls, with the benefits of distance and perspective, "Living under Sam Hall's roof, I had become a thief and a liar. I'd made dangerous friends and knew too damned much of the world for my own good. All of this was directly attributable to my father's influence, it seemed to me, and I was thankful to have escaped it" (276). Living with his mother, despite her addiction, gives Ned stability at home and a level of care that he realizes he had come to miss. He sees his new situation as an advantageous trade; in exchange for giving up his limitless independence, "I again got used to clean sheets, freshly pressed shirts, dinners eaten at a table in the house where I lived" (266). He directs his newfound frustration and self-pity at his once-again-absent father: "I blamed my father, and blamed him most for not looking after me, for not seeing how low I was sinking or for not caring, for not seeing that I deserved better" (276). The interesting narrative maneuver here comes from the perspective of the mature narrator; with years to ponder his childhood, he removes himself from the immediate experiences of Ned the boy and arrives at the conclusion that during that period with Sam he was a miserable and mistreated child. This moment offers an interesting contrast in the narrative perspective of the boy versus the man he becomes; although there were plenty of occasions when young Ned felt uncomfortable or even embarrassed by his father, he never suggests, while living with Sam, that he feels himself sinking, or that his father did not care about him, or that he deserved better. It is only after this part of his life is over, and he has had time to process many of these memories, that his understanding of his own life shifts from that of collaborating with his father to becoming a victim of his father's casual, even careless parenting.

In *The Risk Pool*, Russo carries forward another theme begun in *Mohawk*: the failure of parents and children to communicate effectively. For years Ned struggles to understand how to communicate meaningfully with his father and how to answer his father's inevitable and, to his mind, indecipherable question, "Well?" Although they communicate better with time and proximity and Ned revels in the rare moments when he feels in tune with his father's rhythms, they never really become adept at talking to one another. Late in the story a more mature Ned ponders this element of their relationship: "I'd gotten over, long ago, my father's need to have third parties around when we faced the prospect of a long period of time in each other's company. I hadn't figured out what it meant and didn't want to, though I think I'd always known that we were both afraid. If we had too much time and too little to do, we'd be tempted to talk to each other. Say things. About then, and now, and why, and why not" (410). Many of the children in Russo's fiction who struggle to communicate with their parents also seem to be struggling with the effort not to turn into versions of them. Ned repeatedly sees Tria as just a younger version of her mother, and after Leigh, Ned's future wife, returns from a frustrating visit with her family, she states, "I don't want to be my mother. I want to be who I want to be" (460). This same guilty inarticulation later resurfaces in *Nobody's Fool*, this time from the father's point of view as Sully wonders why he has such a hard time talking to and understanding his grown son.

As in his first novel, Russo again portrays the town of Mohawk as a community fallen on hard times; except for Jack Ward, who marries into wealth,

F. William Peterson, a lawyer living a bit further away from the economic cliff than most, and, at the end, Sam's newfound cadre of professional buddies, few characters seem economically stable. The narrative focuses on the town's hard-working and hard-pressed residents who scrabble to make a living through seasonal road construction (as Sam Hall does), service work in restaurants or bars (such as Alice and Eileen), or other modest, low-skilled jobs (Jenny Hall is a telephone operator, Tree is a park attendant, and Marion is a prostitute). Despite the absence of main characters working in the tanneries, it is these "skin mills" that represent the center of Mohawk's faltering economy. Unfortunately this center cannot hold; the narrator explains, "The tanneries—the town's lifeblood—conceded to be in temporary decline before the war, began to close down after its completion, victims of foreign competition and local greed. While the men who worked in the shops waited for them to reopen, the owners, those who hadn't moved to Florida with their profits and the faith of Mohawk's men and women, were working diligently to keep other industry out of the county, thereby ensuring that Mohawk would remain destitute even in the midst of postwar prosperity" (68). Most residents appear trapped in this hopeless web; furthermore, they are so deeply rooted in place that they cannot imagine moving away and starting over.

This failure of imagination is represented perhaps most poignantly in Jenny Hall's dreams of living somewhere warm and far away, especially after speaking to other telephone operators in Tucson or Albuquerque or San Diego, "where they capitalized the word Summer" (6). But lacking both the means and the wherewithal to relocate, Jenny never seems to see the Southwest as a legitimate possibility; Ned even concludes that "she didn't truly believe in the existence of Tucson, Arizona, or perhaps didn't believe that her personal seasons would be significantly altered by geographical considerations. She had inherited my grandfather's modest house, and that rooted her to the spot" (6). This theme runs throughout much of Russo's fiction: people struggle to makes ends meet in their battered little towns, but through a lack of imagination, education, employment opportunities, will, or some combination thereof, they seldom succeed at leaving these towns behind. Ned offers an unusual example of a relocated, or dislocated, Mohawk native, as he ends up working as an editor in New York City. The end of the novel, however, raises significant questions about whether he ever succeeds at separating himself, emotionally, from his hometown.

The context of economically depressed Mohawk and its downtrodden citizens offers Russo the opportunity to examine closely issues of socioeconomic class. In *The Risk Pool* he chooses to portray socioeconomic class strictly from the bottom up; his perspective is that of a small boy from the working class who gradually grows up and learns firsthand the intense longing and perpetual frustration that are tied to a lack of class mobility and access to money. Indeed part of Ned's coming-of-age story has to do with his growing awareness of class distinctions that start out largely invisible or irrelevant to him but become increasingly visible and significant. For much of the novel the Wards, among Mohawk's few wealthy families, serve as the catalysts for Ned's evolving understanding of class. For example, as a twelve-year-old, Ned faces a never-before-considered conundrum: according to his father, Jack Ward has more money than he can spend. This strikes Ned as "an interesting problem to have" (105), and he uses this information to reevaluate his own family's financial situation. Until this point he had believed that his mother's income of forty dollars a week made them "pretty well-to-do. Maybe there wasn't money for everything we wanted, but I had figured that was a pretty universal condition. Other people couldn't be all that much better off" (105). He knows that his father's economic solvency ebbs and flows with the seasons; Sam is flush during the spring and summer, when he works on the road crews, and strapped during the winter, when his unemployment checks dwindle and it is too cold to work outside. Ned sees nothing particularly unusual about this arrangement, but the presence of the Ward family in Mohawk contributes to his nascent understanding of a bigger economic picture, one less dependent on the seasonal vagaries of construction work or factory labor.

Ned's youthful obsession with the Wards' "white jewel house" becomes a controlling metaphor throughout the novel for the working class's endless fascination with the wealthy. Having absolutely no acquaintance with wealth, Ned wonders "what sort of people lived there, and what it must be like to wake up in such a big house, and what they thought about when they looked out from their vast privacy across the highway into the wild green of Myrtle Park." Then his musings become more pessimistic, and he thinks that "maybe they didn't look in my direction at all. Maybe way off beyond them was another gleaming house on another hill with an even better view, and maybe they looked at that. Or it could be that they just drew the blinds and didn't go gazing off anywhere." The boy's conclusion, however, firmly establishes his belief in the notion that money necessarily equals happiness: "Whoever they were, they had to be pretty happy about things" (98).

He is surprised to learn that his father knows Jack Ward, the owner of the house, and finds it hard to believe that, despite their shared experiences fighting in World War II, the two very different men could possibly have anything in common. Although Ned has seen Jack Ward many times from afar, Ward appears up close for the first time when he and his daughter Tria inexplicably show up at the Elms restaurant. Ned recalls, "He was dressed wonderfully, like somebody from another part of the world who'd come to a modest party expecting an extravagant one" (170). This suggestion that Ward comes "from another part of the world" is certainly true in a socio-economic sense, if not a geographic one. This brief encounter with Ward and his beautiful daughter initiates a significant change in Ned's perception of his station in life. After leaving the Elms, Ned and his father head for the more familiar (and affordable) Empire Grill, where Ned's dinner consists of French fries and gravy. As Ned looks around the diner and its few customers, he thinks morosely, "Everything looked shabby, somehow. Shabbier than usual. And when Wild Bill used his index finger to scour the last drop of dirty coffee from the bottom of his cup, I wanted to cry" (173). Suddenly he can see himself and his life through Jack and Tria Ward's eyes, and for the first time he is humbled and ashamed by what he sees.

This incident does not mark the last time, though, that an encounter with the Wards alters Ned's perspective on wealth. Later in the novel, when Ned returns to Mohawk after being away at college, he is stunned to see how his perception of wealth and class has changed. After accepting a chance invitation from Mrs. Ward to join her and her daughter for brunch, Ned drives up the winding road and then, catching a glimpse of the house, stops short. He notes in amazement, "The white jewel house was little more than a big, fancy ranch of the sort that sat side by side awaiting mature foliage, in the better Tucson housing developments. It was not nearly as nice as the house of the English professor whose house I'd played poker in the night before I left the city" (322). Ned is completely unprepared for this dramatic upending of his long-held belief in the Wards' absolute wealth and the notion that their lives were immeasurably different from anything he could comprehend.

This new awareness that the Wards are not so different from other people he had come to know allows Ned, later, to approach Tria romantically. After they spend a single night together, however, Ned finds himself pulling away from her. He spends the evening drinking with his father and his father's best friend, Wussy, instead of taking Tria out to dinner, as he had promised. Ned feels himself becoming one of the men of Mohawk whose lives are marked by alcoholism, irresponsibility, and poor decision making. Ned, however, occupies the unusual position of actually having an opportunity to achieve a certain measure of success, through his education, his experience beyond the circumscribed world of Mohawk, and even his potential for a relationship with Tria. But at this point, he feels completely unwilling to extricate himself from the rhythms of his father's life, the rhythms that he finally understands after many years of confusion. These evenings of feeling perfectly in sync with his father's rhythm, Ned remembers, "were magic for me, and they made me grin at him so stupidly, so drunkenly, so affectionately, that I had all I could do not to tell him that we were becoming simpatico" (375).

Sam Hall and his crowd seem to think of Jack Ward's life as entirely disconnected from their own; although the topic of the local rich man remains fascinating to them, his primary usefulness to them is as the target of their jokes, especially how he died "in the saddle" with a much younger woman on the golf course (248). But Drew Littler's obsession with the Wards exists on an entirely different level. The conviction, perhaps justifiable, that he is Jack Ward's biological son and therefore will someday inherit the white jewel house and all its associated wealth fuels Drew's life. Like a child dreaming that he is really a prince and will someday be rescued from his awful life that he does not deserve, Drew becomes utterly committed to this fairy-tale version of his future. As he and Ned gaze at the white house on the hill, he tells Ned confidently, "This house is going to be mine someday" (114). Ned bristles at Drew's presumption and thinks, "I felt like telling him that he was nuts to think he'd ever own a house like this one, any more than I would. It was dumb to kid himself" (114). What Ned will not realize until much later is that Drew intends not to buy a house something like the Wards' but rather to inherit that actual house as Jack Ward's eldest child and only son.

His plans for inheritance notwithstanding, Drew Littler cultivates what the narrator terms a "personal philosophy of life" (152) that leads him to organize Ned and another boy, Willie Heinz, in a three-man organization designed "to abuse rich people, all of whom Drew hated with a white-hot passion. The 'Money People' he called them, the people who thought they were too good, who considered themselves above the rest." According to Drew, "it was the fault of the people who had money that those who hadn't any lived difficult lives" (152). Drew's attitude toward money differs dramatically from the passivity common to many of Russo's other working-class characters. Some hard-pressed workers persist in remaining grateful to the tannery bosses for giving them a way to make their livings. Others, disenchanted with the prospects of regular work, gravitate toward the poker table or the OTB, believing that eventually the cards will fall their way or that their daily double is bound to hit. Drew, deranged as he may be, is unusual in Russo's fiction for actually dreaming bigger and for taking some action, misguided though it is, to address the disparity of wealth and privilege in dying factory or mill towns such as Mohawk. The rueful irony of his ill-formed plans, though, is that "there were so few people in Mohawk with any real money. Since the tanneries had begun closing down, the county had gotten progressively poorer, and most of the men who had made their money in leather had taken it with them to Florida." But, as the narrator notes, "for Drew Littler you could qualify as one of the Money People if you had a picture window in the living room or a Doughboy pool in the backyard. It was from Drew that I learned the ultimate relativity of wealth—that wealthy people are those who have a dollar more than you do" (151–52).

Many of the Mohawk men who ponder the difference between their lives and that of Jack Ward come to the conclusion that it all boils down to luck. If their luck had been different, goes this logic, then they would be the ones married to rich wives, living in fancy houses, and driving Lincolns while Jack Ward spends his last dollar on beers in a grungy bar. The notion of luck surfaces with some regularity in *The Risk Pool*; the town of Mohawk is generally deemed to be unlucky, merely by virtue of its shuttered mills and high unemployment. And Ned encounters periodic situations when an individual's luck is invoked as the explanation for whatever the current reality may be. When Ned is a college student, his roommate accuses him of being lucky because his draft number is so high. Later, while sitting on the Wards' patio eating brunch with Tria and enjoying the feeling of falling in love with her, Ned feels lucky and attributes this luck to his ability, inherited from his father, to walk away from things, in this case his dysfunctional life in Tucson.

Sam believes even more passionately in the existence of luck, and he says to Ned, after denying the possibility that the Ward family could possibly be broke, "Some people are born lucky. You can't do a thing to change it." When Ned disagrees, Sam is not shaken. "Well, it's true whether you believe it or not," he counters. Revisiting this conversation later, Ned muses, "I thought about it all the way home and couldn't decide whether I'd ever met anybody who was truly lucky. The person who came closest, the more I thought about it, was me" (404–5). On the surface this comes as an unexpected comment, as Ned's life seems far from lucky. He has a mother nearly incapacitated by mental illness, a father of questionable value as a role model, a graduate career in ruins, a failed relationship with Tria, barely any money, and few employment prospects. Yet Russo turns this model of outward failure upside down; Ned believes himself to be lucky, and part of his luck resides, perhaps, in his willingness to leave Mohawk behind. In Russo's first novel, *Mohawk,* nearly every main character still alive at the end leaves town. But in *The Risk Pool,* Russo's sensibility about the fate of small-town residents seems to have evolved enough to acknowledge that only a few ever seem to escape and that those who do are forever marked by their experiences.

Shortly after fourteen-year-old Ned returns to his mother's house, the mature narrator addresses the reader directly: "And so began the final stage of my boyhood in Mohawk. Later, as an adult, I would return from time to time. As a visitor, though, never again as a true resident. But then I wouldn't be a true resident of any other place, either, joining instead the great multitude of wandering Americans, so many of whom have a Mohawk in their past, the memory of which propels us we know not precisely where, so long as it's away. Return we do, but only to gain momentum for our next outward arc, each further than the last, until there is no elasticity left, nothing to draw us home" (264–65). At its heart *The Risk Pool* is a story about that elasticity and how time and distance seem to weaken it. The beautiful, elegiac nature of this passage, however, belies the truth of the novel; Russo suggests that some elasticity always remains. Former residents may no longer return to their literal hometown, but the novel invokes a version of an old cliché: you can take the boy out of Mohawk, but you cannot take Mohawk out of the boy. In the final scene of the novel, after Leigh gives birth to a baby boy the same night as Sam's "send-off," Ned's first encounter with his son is depicted in language almost identical to that of the scene in which a young Sam first saw his own baby son. This heavy-handed parallelism seems clearly designed to suggest a cycle of parenthood that may not yet have run its course. Ned seems to have enough self-knowledge and self-awareness to become a thoughtful and loving father. His ability to follow through, however, remains uncertain as the novel draws to a close.

The Risk Pool remains one of Russo's more popular novels, and the author recommends that readers new to his work begin with this one. It serves in many ways as a perfect introduction to the themes that matter most to him. Characters from *The Risk Pool* develop into primary players in subsequent novels; for example, Sam Hall's character evolves to become the slightly more responsible but equally stubborn Donald "Sully" Sullivan in *Nobody's Fool* and then evolves again to become the even less responsible but just as colorful Max Roby in *Empire Falls*. We see a complicated father-son relationship in *The Risk Pool*, told from the son's point of view, that marks the beginning of a long pattern of complicated father-son relationships that are central to *Nobody's Fool, Straight Man, Empire Falls, Bridge of Sighs,* and *That Old Cape Magic*. We see marriages and relationships struggling and failing; Sam and Jenny Hall's rocky marriage presages, among others, Sully and Vera's in *Nobody's Fool,* the elder Devereauxs' in *Straight Man,* Grace and Max's in *Empire Falls,* and those of both sets of Griffins (especially the elder) in *That Old Cape Magic*.

The Risk Pool also establishes a sense that, for Russo's characters, the pain that one experiences, whether physical or emotional, is secondary to how gracefully one handles it. Sam's casual acceptance of his mangled thumb foreshadows Sully's forbearance toward his damaged knee in *Nobody's Fool;* other characters who suffer various infirmities (Hank's urinary problem in *Straight Man,* David's crippled arm in *Empire Falls*) are judged not by the severity of their ailments but by how well they cope with them. Other important narrative patterns established in *The Risk Pool* include the importance of familiar public locations—mostly diners and bars—in the small towns that Russo creates—the Mohawk Grill and the Elms in *The Risk Pool* become Hattie's Lunch and the Horse in *Nobody's Fool,* which in turn become the Empire Grill in *Empire Falls* and Ikey's store in *Bridge of Sighs.* Russo begins to demonstrate in *The Risk Pool* the many ways community develops among people whose homes and families might leave something to be desired; despite many recurring comments about dying alone, for example, when Sam dies at the end of *The Risk Pool,* the whole town turns out to celebrate his life, demonstrating beyond a doubt that he was a vibrant member of a vibrant community. The power and value of community and communal bonds remain fundamental in much of Russo's later fiction.

CHAPTER 4

Nobody's Fool

Richard Russo has often professed his deep admiration for the broad canvases and large casts of long nineteenth-century novels, "because of their ambition, their wanting to see more of the world, their desire not just to look at the interior workings of a single character and situation."[1] This narrative ambition clearly surfaces in his third novel, *Nobody's Fool,* which employs a straight third-person omniscient narrator who closely follows the life of Donald "Sully" Sullivan, a sixty-year-old handyman with a badly injured knee, as he pinballs from job to poker game, courtroom to jail, diner to OTB and back again amid a sea of secondary characters almost too numerous to count. According to Russo, the actual writing of *Nobody's Fool* was "excruciating" because of his long struggle to identify the appropriate narrative approach. "I started it in Sully's voice," he explained in a 1993 interview, "and wrote hundreds of pages before I found that his point of view was too limiting. I wrote a second draft as a series of narrations through various characters' eyes, then I had to throw that away when I realized this was an omniscient book; I needed to be outside all the characters with access to their thoughts."[2]

In *Nobody's Fool,* Russo leaves behind the fictional town of Mohawk, New York, for a new setting, ostensibly just up the road. North Bath bears a number of resemblances to Mohawk; both are out-of-the-way upstate New York towns with small populations and even smaller economic prospects. However, they have significantly different histories. Mohawk carries with it the burden of failed factories and tanneries; its manufacturing workforce remains in place but without a place to work. North Bath, however, was never a manufacturing town. Its history lay in tourism; the discovery of mineral springs in the area led to a population boom in the nineteenth century. As a result a huge resort hotel was built to host thousands of visitors, and a local service industry thrived. But when the springs dried up in 1868, the fortunes of the town dried up just as quickly. In contrast, a nearby town, Schulyer Springs, found its mineral springs to be perfectly stable, and so the economy there flourished. More than a century later, in the mid-1980s, the residents of North Bath still find themselves waiting for their luck to change and cursing the good fortune of their thriving neighbors.

After many decades of stasis in North Bath, the town is in a moment of flux in *Nobody's Fool* as its deeply felt isolation from the rest of the world appears to be about to end. Plans for a giant and controversial amusement park, "The Ultimate Escape," are in the works, and although many residents look to this project as a remedy for the chronic unemployment that drives young people away, others fear the loss of their small-town peacefulness and the disruption of a cemetery near the building site. Yuppies from Albany have begun buying and renovating the once-beautiful, now-decrepit Victorian mansions on Upper Main Street, bringing a new source of revenue to the town but at the same time changing the tenor of the neighborhood. In many ways North Bath appears to be on the cusp of a significant transformation, and so too does Sully, who has spent the last several decades in a relatively steady state.

The story of *Nobody's Fool* takes place over the course of about two months, from the day before Thanksgiving in 1984 until about mid-January 1985. During these weeks the fate of the town and the fortunes of Donald "Sully" Sullivan, the main character, change considerably. Sully is a divorced handyman with a grown son he barely knows, an on-again, off-again relationship with a married waitress named Ruth, and a seething hatred for his late father, who was a drunk, abusive manipulator. Sully occupies an almost-empty apartment above the home of Mrs. Beryl Peoples, an eighty-year-old retired English teacher, whose son, Clive Jr., is the president of the local bank and the person responsible for the development of "The Ultimate Escape." Sully has been awarded partial disability support because of a serious knee injury, and as a condition of his payments the court has ordered him to take classes (in refrigeration and air-conditioning repair) at the local community college in order to retrain for work that he is physically able to do. But Sully, whose stubborn streak appears early and often in this novel, instead turns to his dim-witted best pal, Rub Squeers, to assist him as he returns to working construction, under the table, for Carl Roebuck. Also complicating Sully's personal landscape is his bitter adult son, Peter, a history professor, who returns to North Bath after being denied tenure and whose marriage is rapidly falling apart. But the presence of Peter's timorous young son Will seems to offer Sully a chance to redeem himself, in some ways, for his neglectful parenting by becoming a kind and (relatively) attentive grandfather.

This novel's title, *Nobody's Fool,* is a punning reference to Sully, who in the traditional sense of the phrase truly is nobody's fool. Sully is smart and confident, and he exhibits a remarkable dexterity in dealing with people in difficult situations. These character traits allow him to cultivate many friends and few enemies, and he is not someone easily taken advantage of. However, at the age of sixty Sully finds himself "divorced from his own wife, carrying on halfheartedly with another man's, estranged from his son, devoid of self-knowledge, badly crippled and virtually unemployable—all of which he stubbornly confuse[s] with independence" (25). So he is also the other kind of "nobody's fool"—that is, a fool who belongs to nobody. Inept at maintaining romantic relationships and unsure how to resurrect his parental relationship with his son, from the outside at least Sully appears to be profoundly alone in the world. Russo, however, demonstrates once again that a man without a wife or a traditional family need not feel alone.

Critics generally responded positively to *Nobody's Fool,* though many noted that the novel was somewhat longer than it needed to be. The novelist Francine Prose, in her *New York Times* review, praised the novel for its engaging characters and appealing qualities: "Mr. Russo deals with interesting themes (he'd have to, in all these pages): change and stasis, free will and obligation, luck, responsibility, forgiveness—the bonds of community, friendship, and family." Later in the review, however, she criticized the novel for being too lengthy, with excessive subplots and minor characters, and chided Russo for not being a tougher editor of his own work.[3] John Skow, writing in the pages of *Time* magazine, offered a slightly more negative view of *Nobody's Fool,* claiming that "the author's approach to character . . . is that of commedia dell'arte. He assigns an easily recognizable peculiarity to each actor in his masque, who then exhibits his oddity whenever he is in view." The result is an enjoyable but perhaps overly predictable read. "Most of the time it works," Skow nevertheless conceded, "not so much because the author keeps things stirred up but because he persuades the reader to share his great, openhearted fondness for his ridiculous characters."[4]

In a much more overtly positive review, published in *Antioch Review,* Steve Brzezinski openly admired Russo's ambitious and compassionate tackling of class and small-town America, two themes that he noted are "currently out of favor in American literature." He applauded *Nobody's Fool* for its "completely believable fictional landscape peopled with assorted charlatans, buffoons, and chronic underachievers, all of whom [Russo] succeeds in making us care passionately about through the sheer force of the narrative."

Brzezinski went on to note, "[Russo's] characters, like Samuel Beckett's, are inevitably falling down, but they always get up, only to fall down again. Russo would say it is not merely the getting up that makes people truly human, but the falling down as well. This dialectic between occasional triumph and inevitable catastrophe gives the book an unusual texture, both bleak and cheerful at the same time."[5] A *Times Literary Supplement* review described the "lovable eccentrics" who populate *Nobody's Fool* and placed Russo's work "in a broad tradition of American nostalgia, one encompassing figures as diverse as Twain, Sherwood Anderson, Faulkner and Garrison Keillor (perhaps Russo's closest contemporary)."[6]

In *Nobody's Fool*, Russo extends several of the themes so central to his previous novel *The Risk Pool*, including the intersection of place and class, the relationships between fathers and sons, and the role of community. As in *Mohawk* and *The Risk Pool*, women characters feature significantly in *Nobody's Fool* but do not occupy the most prominent roles. Cass is a lifelong friend to Sully, and the two of them behave like brother and sister, even to the point of sharing responsibility for the care of Cass's senile, elderly mother, Hattie. Ruth and, to a lesser extent, her daughter, Janey, and granddaughter, Tina, figure in an important subplot of the novel, but one much subordinated to Sully's primary story. Toby Roebuck, Carl's wife, is beautiful, unhappy, and married to Sully's boss; Sully's abiding crush on her provides him with something of a hobby, but she remains on the periphery of his story. Other women characters skate in and out of the novel; the demented Hattie propels segments of the plot forward, first by escaping her booth at the diner and prompting Sully to rescue her, and then by dying in a freak cash register accident. Janey, Ruth's daughter, tries to avoid her abusive husband, Roy (a native of Mohawk, incidentally), by hiding out at Sully's house several times, but she seldom actually encounters Sully.

By far the most prominent female character, and one of Russo's most engaging women characters in all his novels, is Mrs. Beryl Peoples. She contributes directly to Sully's story insofar as she is his current landlord, former teacher, and perpetual mother figure; she has known and cared about him for most of his life. Near the end of the novel, she pays the back taxes that Sully owes on his father's decrepit house, thus saving the property for Sully and providing him with a much-needed source of income. Despite being the most intelligent character in the cast, Mrs. Peoples is also one of the more eccentric (and that is saying something). Although she lives alone, she talks almost constantly, directing her comments either to Clive Sr., her late husband, whose photograph sits on the television, or to Ed, an African Zamble mask hung on the wall. Her hilarious insights regarding her neighbor Mrs.

Gruber and her general role as interpreter of North Bath culture make her indispensable to the novel. Her conflicted feelings about her son, for whom she lacks typical parental love, portrayed alongside her abiding affection for Sully, whom she loves like a son, illuminate another of Russo's important themes: the true definition of family is not limited to blood relations. Mrs. Peoples makes an effort to be kind and loving toward Clive Jr., but she clearly feels a deeper and more natural maternal affection for Sully.

In the end the true stars of *Nobody's Fool* are the male characters, and Sully is clearly the headliner. Like Sam Hall in *The Risk Pool,* Sully has no home life to speak of, and he spends his time almost exclusively in public places. His days are bookended by breakfast at Hattie's Lunch and late-night beers at the Horse sitting next to his lawyer, Wirf, and baiting Tiny, the grouchy bartender; in between he works (when he can), bets his trifecta at the OTB, plays poker, helps out at Hattie's, and otherwise hangs around with his male friends in places that quickly become as comfortable and familiar to readers as they are to Sully. When asked by an interviewer in 1993 about the significance of Sully's various "homes"—the diner, the OTB, the bar—Russo responded:

> Place is inseparable from character. If I try to write books about people before I have a pretty good sense of the places, that's an indication that I don't know the characters as well as I need to. And it's crucial to have a sense of place as process. Sully going to Hattie's first, then the OTB, then the Horse; the rhythms of his life are inseparable from who he is and what he thinks of himself. That comes from some of the real loves of my life in terms of literature, Dickens first and foremost: how do we know Pip in *Great Expectations,* except in terms of the forge, the blacksmith's shop and the marsh? Many of the contemporary writers I like also have that feeling of the way in which places and people interact.[7]

Sully's many places do not include a home in the conventional sense; he rents an apartment in Mrs. Peoples's house only so he will have a place to sleep and shower, and he seldom spends any time there. Indeed there appears to be no good reason for Sully to spend time at home, in an almost literally empty apartment, when all of the people he cares about are elsewhere. His strong connections with his close friends, including Rub, Carl Roebuck, Wirf, and by the end of the novel even his son, Peter, all develop in public places. Other friends he encounters in his various haunts, including Jocko, Ollie, Harold, and Ralph, serve to round out Sully's surprisingly vibrant and sustaining social network. Although Sully genuinely cares for Ruth and for Mrs.

Peoples and he enjoys flirting with Toby, romantic or familial connections are not the fuel that powers his life, and his most important personal ties are with the North Bath men with whom he works, drinks, and gambles.

Sully's enduring relationships with men make a certain amount of sense, given that romantic relationships between men and women in *Nobody's Fool* are fraught with misery. Nearly every character is divorced, widowed, or unhappily married; not a single healthy, happy relationship exists between the men and women of the story. This world of miserable relationships is not new to Russo's fiction; *Mohawk* is rife with failed or unhappy marriages, and in *The Risk Pool* the twice-married Jenny Hall gives voice to this apparently futile search for meaningful connection when she plaintively expresses her dream of finding "my own true love." Her son, the narrator in that novel, responds in amazement, thinking that her wish was one "that everyone had a right to, but that only the very foolish or the terminally naïve trouble themselves over" (313). This notion that true love is something for the foolish or the naive carries over into *Nobody's Fool*; characters are motivated by money, by pride, by greed, by stubbornness, and even by lust, but seldom by romantic love.

This is not to suggest that *Nobody's Fool* is a novel devoid of love; in fact the opposite is true. The novel may lack examples of satisfying romantic love or even companionate love, but it is full of the love found in true friendship. Sully loves Wirf and Rub and Mrs. Peoples and Cass and even Ruth, in his own way, and they love him in return. He even feels a "powerful . . . affection mixed with aggravation" (488) toward Carl Roebuck, his sometime employer. Love among family members, though, is quite a bit harder to come by in this novel. Sully's relationships with his parents and his brother, now all long dead, were fractious at best and deeply abusive at worst. His feelings for his ex-wife lean more toward amazement that they were ever married at all, given their profound lack of compatibility. He has lived for three decades with scarcely a thought for his son and certainly without any emotional attachment to him. But by the end of the novel, his relationship with Peter has begun to develop into one that includes respect and may well evolve into some form of genuine parental love. Clearer is the bond that Sully forges with his grandson Will, who at first reminds him of the frustrating, scared little boy Peter used to be but who quickly begins to earn Sully's genuine affection. Sully even acknowledges to himself his unexpected love for the boy and marvels at "this tightness of the heart he felt for his grandson, as if some natural, biological affection were coming to him late, after skipping a generation" (321). With the important exception of Will, Sully does not openly express his love for others in his life, but the narrator makes clear that the love Sully feels for his friends sustains and protects him from what would otherwise be an overwhelmingly lonely life.

Although Sully may be capable of love, he can be oblivious when it comes to expressing his feelings. In contrast, Rub Squeers may be one of the dumbest, smelliest, oddest-looking sidekicks ever imagined, but he is also the only character in *Nobody's Fool* who seems able to love without reservation or qualification. His adoration for Sully is unmatched by any other emotion in his life (his feelings for his shrewish caricature of a wife, Bootsie, certainly do not register as real love), and he suffers tremendous jealousy when Peter and Will begin to co-opt some of Sully's precious attention. He struggles to maintain what he fears is his precarious position as Sully's best friend, and when at one point Sully pushes him too far and Rub walks away in anger and frustration, readers know that Rub's heart has been broken, even if Sully does not. Peter gives Rub the nickname "Sancho," a name that Rub hates and does not understand and that provides readers with a brilliant flash of understated literary humor that evokes Sancho Panza, Don Quixote's loyal but simple sidekick. Loyal Rub proves to be, for even after Sully humiliates him in an odd scene that involves Sully stubbornly following Rub in a truck down a residential sidewalk, in the end Rub forgives his friend and tearfully accepts Sully's simple but truthful explanation that "[Peter] is my son. You're my best friend" (500).

As much as Russo focuses on the power and importance of friendship in *Nobody's Fool,* at its heart this novel, like many of Russo's others, is really an examination of father-son relationships. In *The Risk Pool,* Russo explores an unusual relationship between a neglectful father and his son over the course of some thirty years, told entirely from the son's first-person point of view. But in *Nobody's Fool,* Russo's vision expands outward to encompass multiple generations of fathers and sons. Although Sully's evolving relationship with Peter is arguably at the center of the novel, his complicated and still-painful relationship with his own father, the abusive Big Jim Sullivan, provides the backdrop for all Sully's musings on parenting. Big Jim Sullivan brutalized his son, beating and torturing the boy in order to establish who was "boss" in their house. "You can fight me all you want," his father threatened Sully, "but you aren't going to win" (277). Years later, when his own son was born, Sully took an entirely different approach to bad parenting: "Instead of abusing Peter, he'd ignored the boy, forgotten him for months at a stretch" (175). Nevertheless, Peter undoubtedly fares better than either Sully or Big Jim did, given the loving presence of his stepfather, Ralph. But after Peter became a father, he essentially abandoned his eldest son, Will, a timid, sensitive boy, to the sociopathic behaviors of his younger son, Wacker. Peter never really believed that Wacker could hurt Will, but "pain was Wacker's business," and Will had to remain constantly, stressfully vigilant against Wacker's assaults, relaxing "only when his brother was asleep" (168). As a result of Peter's careless lack of protection and Wacker's cruel intimidation and assaults, Will actually exhibits many symptoms commonly associated with stress disorders. This fourth generation of Sullivan boys seems destined to suffer, yet again, for a father's inadequacies, until the final chapters begin to suggest a path toward redemption for Sully, Peter, and Will.

In typical Russo fashion, Nobody's Fool establishes that even when fathers set the parenting bar pathetically low, somehow mothers still fail to shine by comparison. Vera, Sully's ex-wife, pours her heart into making sure that their son, Peter, does not turn into his father; she sacrifices to keep them apart, even sending Peter away to boarding school in order to prevent Sully from taking an interest in the boy. (She realizes, too late, that her fears were completely unfounded.) Yet by the end of the novel, her worst nightmare has materialized; she has somehow lost this futile, one-sided, vindictive parenting competition to the completely disengaged Sully. "You won," she tells Sully bitterly, admitting, "I've loved [Peter] until my heart broke right in two. You could care less, so you're the one he wants" (361). Although Sully denies both the existence of the competition and his status as winner, the reader understands that Vera is essentially correct. Although Peter clings tenaciously to his long-held resentments toward his father, he also begins to acknowledge his growing bond with him and even entertains the possibility "that he was not so different from his natural father as he'd always liked to think" (295). This element of Nobody's Fool echoes a similar theme in The Risk Pool, in that both Vera and Jenny Hall do their best to educate their sons, raise them right, and inspire in them the goal of being different men than their fathers are. Tellingly, both mothers have good reasons to doubt their success.

Both Vera and Jenny Hall might well attribute their ex-husbands' magnetism to simple luck, but in Russo's novels luck is critical but never simple. Like several of his other novels, Nobody's Fool wrestles with questions of luck and how much of one's fate really relies on luck to the exclusion of talent, merit, effort, or other qualities. The novel opens with a description of North Bath, a town whose residents believe that "if it weren't for bad luck they wouldn't have any at all." Their town's history pivots on the moment when the local mineral springs, a profitable draw for tourists, "began, like luck, to dry up and with them the town's wealth and future" (7). Nearly a century later the ramshackle town "was still waiting for its luck to change. There were encouraging signs. A restored Sans Souci, what was left of it, was scheduled to reopen in the summer, and a new spring had been success-fully drilled on the hotel's extensive grounds. And luck, so the conventional wisdom went, ran in cycles" (9). In the first chapter, Russo establishes a setting where the vagaries of luck take precedence over all other paths to success, where things just seem to happen, rather than determined people making them happen. This atmosphere crystallizes in the scenes in which Mrs. Peoples and her neighbors stare fearfully upward into the branches of the dying elms that line their street, feeling victimized by fate and wondering helplessly when their luck will run out and a limb will crash down onto the homes below.

Sully is deeply invested in the idea of luck, and not just when it comes to betting on horse races (though luck does play an important role in that endeavor). He believes that Carl Roebuck was "threatening to use up, singlehandedly, all the luck there was left in an unlucky town" (41); his lot-tery winnings, beautiful wife, successful business, and general good fortune suggest that Carl is a "man [who] could shit in a swinging bucket" (42). At one point, while he was still in jail, Sully asked Peter directly if he believed in luck; Peter denied it, and Sully "nodded, suspecting as much. 'You know what? I do'" (461), he told Peter. Throughout the novel Sully steadily ref-erences luck as a legitimate explanation for just about any circumstance. He believes in luck as an ambient power that surrounds everything, but he also takes superstitious precautions when he can, trying to exercise his own power over the forces of luck. Upon joining a poker game with Carl and Wirf, for example, "Sully sat, then stood again and walked around his chair, clockwise first, then counterclockwise, to dispel the afternoon's bad luck. 'Red River round a green monkey's asshole,' he added, making a complicated sign in the air over a deck of cards" (259). The magic incantation proves ineffective, for Sully at least, as he leaves the card game several hundred dollars in the hole. Later, Carl scoffs at Sully, "You're the only man I know who believes in luck," to which Sully responds, "I believed in intelligence and hard work until I met you. Only luck explains you." When Carl retorts, "That still leaves your own self with no good explanation," Sully grins and quickly counters, "*Bad* luck explains me" (328–29). Luck, whether the good luck enjoyed by Carl Roebuck or the bad luck endured by Sully, seems to provide the answer to nearly every question.

The answers to some of the novel's other questions, however, seem to reside not in luck, whether good or bad, but rather in more metaphysical concepts of fate and free will. When the court orders Sully to take classes at the local community college as part of a job-retraining effort, he finds himself in a philosophy class when the vocational classes are filled. Despite feeling foolish for enrolling in a class full of teenagers, Sully enjoys the philosophy course, and his young professor's lectures about the illusion of free will repeatedly echo in his mind. He is amazed at his young professor, who "seemed bent on disproving everything in the world, one thing at a time" (27). Over time Sully comes to believe that the professor's goal is to make everything disappear, "and then replace all of it with something new, a new kind of thought or existence maybe. . . . And maybe this wasn't such a bad idea if you were talking to twenty-year-olds. . . . But now, at sixty, he was less willing to throw things away that could be patched together and kept running for a few more months. He wanted to keep going forward, not stop and turn around and analyze the validity of decisions made and courses charted long ago" (76–77).

Within Sully's response to his philosophy class lies all of his reluctance to revisit past decisions and to indulge in regret over how his life has turned out. At times he feels surrounded by people (mostly women) intent on making him feel regretful; Ruth repeatedly admonishes him about a decision he made years ago not to go into business with Carl Roebuck's father, Kenny, and reproaches him for never reconciling with his father. Beryl Peoples even asks him pointedly, "Does it ever bother you that you haven't done more with the life God gave you?," to which Sully replies, "Not often" and then adds, tellingly, "Now and then" (130–31). It is clear that Sully does drift toward regretfulness, at least "now and then," even though, as the narrator emphatically asserts, Sully "didn't see much margin in regret" and had "decided long ago to abstain from all but the most general forms of regret" (253). Deciding such a thing, though, does not necessarily make it so; Sully deems specific regrets strictly off-limits, and yet he finds it difficult to maintain this distance from past mistakes. Still he tries, even to the point of denying Rub the apology he clearly deserves, because apologizing "could conceivably open the floodgates to other forms of regret" (491).

Over time Sully thinks more and more about his philosophy professor's lectures, the supposed illusion of free will, and the notion of an interconnected world. None of the other courses he takes at the community college has nearly the influence of this philosophy class, which seems to provide Sully with some of the abstract ideas he needs to help him make sense of his current situation. For example, one of the "cockamamie theories" espoused by his professor was that "everybody, all the people in the world, were linked by invisible strings, and when you moved you were really exerting influence on other people. Even if you couldn't see the strings pulling, they were there just the same. At the time Sully had considered the idea bullshit" (329). But by the end of the novel, he starts to acknowledge and even appreciate the ways in which his life interconnects in important ways with those around him. He feels the bonds of family through his relationship with Will, feels concern and apprehension when he learns Wirf has been diagnosed with cancer, and feels responsibility for his aging landlady. He seems to surprise even himself with the long list of tasks and obligations he hands over to Peter to manage while he is in jail over Christmas—help out at Hattie's, finish the floor at the Roebucks' camp, lend Rub a dollar for his daily bet, hitch up the snowplow if it snows, feed Rasputin the dog. "Maybe there were strings," he thinks. "Maybe you caused things even when you tried hard not to" (330).

This newfound awareness of his role in other people's lives marks perhaps the most important change that Sully experiences throughout *Nobody's Fool.* Instead of seeing himself as a loner who has no significant impact on those around him, he begins to appreciate the many ways that he and the members of his community rely on one another. Furthermore, Sully opens himself up to the possibility of embracing his roles as a father and a grandfather, choosing to cultivate a long-term relationship with both Peter and Will.

Although Sully's emotional life may have changed over the course of the novel, outwardly his situation is much the same as it was in the beginning: his knee is still badly damaged; he still owes money on his truck; he still lives in the same empty apartment. Even though Cass has moved away and Ruth has moved on, Sully's circle of male friends remains solidly in place and has now expanded by one, it seems, with the addition of his son, Peter. The novel seems poised at the beginning to encompass sweeping changes in the town and its residents, but in the end both North Bath and Sully remain remarkably intact. "The Ultimate Escape" enterprise falls through after a startling rejection by one of the financiers, who candidly explains to Clive Peoples that his company seeks a different "ambience" in which to locate its amusement park: "A lot of the people up in your neck of the woods behave funny. Hell, Clive, no offense, but they look funny. . . . You got yourself some real beautiful country up there, and I mean that. Nice trees especially. But you also got yourself some people who look like they live in trees, and that's the cruel goddamn truth" (445). The overall sense, though, is that the failure of the amusement park has most dramatically affected Clive Peoples, who escapes town before the news breaks, and perhaps Carl Roebuck, who nevertheless will likely land on his lucky feet. But North Bath will endure, as it has for decades, still the poor cousin to Schuyler Springs, still waiting for its luck to change.

In 1994 Paramount Pictures adapted *Nobody's Fool* into a feature film starring Paul Newman, Bruce Willis, Melanie Griffith, and Jessica Tandy in her last movie role before her death later that year. Russo, who was engaged in the movie's production, was impressed by the effort Newman put into really trying to understand Sully's character. In a 2010 interview, Russo recalled that when he arrived for the first time on the set of *Nobody's Fool*, Newman pulled him aside and began grilling him about Sully's character. "When Sully's alone in his truck, what kind of music does he listen to?" Newman asked Russo, and Russo had to admit, "I didn't really have any answers for him. I had no idea what kind of music Sully would listen to. Everything I know about that guy was in the book, and it wasn't like there were outtakes that I could sweep up from the floor."[8] But Russo clearly admired Newman's commitment to the role and his ability to encapsulate, in a look or a phrase, the trauma of Sully's abusive childhood and the bewilderment he felt at being suddenly drawn into his adult son's life for the first time. The film received two Academy Award nominations, one for Robert Benton for best screenplay based on previously published material and the other for Paul Newman, who played the role of Sully, for best actor in a leading role.

CHAPTER 5

Straight Man

In a 1999 article for the *New York Times* magazine, Richard Russo explained that while on his *Straight Man* book tour, the most common question he encountered was how much he had exaggerated his portrayal of academic life. "By the end of the tour," he recounted, "I had my deadpan response down pat: 'What exaggeration?' If the depiction of lunacy happens to be your goal, academic life requires no embellishment. . . . The challenge, rather, is to tone things down sufficiently so that generous readers outside the academy will find the events credible."[1] Russo certainly had ample time to become well acquainted with the "lunacy" of higher education; his career in academia began in graduate school at the University of Arizona and included teaching positions at Pennsylvania State University–Altoona, Southern Connecticut State University, Southern Illinois University at Carbondale, and, finally, Colby College. His career as an English professor allowed him to draw from his own firsthand experiences with department squabbles, incompetent administrators, ever-looming budget cuts, and marginally prepared students. All of these come into play in *Straight Man*, Russo's only academic satire and a work he considers his "long goodbye to the academy."[2]

Straight Man marks a dramatic departure from Russo's first three novels, all of which are set in upstate New York and take as subjects the struggles of working-class men in deteriorating factory towns. *Straight Man*, in contrast, takes place in the invented rural town of Railton, Pennsylvania, and focuses on Professor Henry William "Hank" Devereaux Jr., a middle-aged English professor at the fictional West Central Pennsylvania University. Departing from his more familiar setting of crumbling tanneries and poisoned streams, Russo instead provides a similarly modest but quite different world of an undistinguished regional state university in a town where the geography seems dominated by run-down rail yards, grungy bars, and various competing sub-divisions, one of which, Allegheny Wells, is home to Hank and his family.

As an academic satire, *Straight Man* falls on a long and rich continuum of works dealing with the foibles of academic life. The earliest example of an American campus novel, Nathaniel Hawthorne's *Fanshawe* (1828), was not particularly successful, but the campus novel quickly gained momentum as a popular genre. By the first decades of the twentieth century, best-selling works such as F. Scott Fitzgerald's *This Side of Paradise* (1920) and Percy Marks's *The Plastic Age* (1924) helped to define youth culture for a general reading audience. Until about the middle of the twentieth century, most campus novels focused primarily on the experiences of students attending university. After World War II, however, academic novels began to divert attention toward the lives of faculty, and critics often cite Mary McCarthy's *The Groves of Academe* (1952), Randall Jarrell's *Pictures From an Institution* (1953), and Kingsley Amis's *Lucky Jim* (1953) as three early touchstones of this focal shift. More recently the emphasis on faculty in academic novels has, in many cases, zeroed in even more specifically on tenure and the ramifications of the tenure process. *Straight Man* falls clearly into this subgenre. In fact Eric Leuschner comments, "Richard Russo's *Straight Man* has in many ways become the heir to Amis's *Lucky Jim* as the contemporary exemplar of the academic novel with its intertwining of budget concerns, tenure problems, and theory wars."[3] Russo even nods to Amis's novel through Hank's nom de plume for his local newspaper op-ed pieces, "Lucky Hank." *Straight Man* appeared amid a flurry of other academic novels in the 1990s; many of these, as Elaine Showalter notes in *Faculty Towers* (2005), "satirized this new cast of characters and their struggles for tenure, status, and political correctness; the tone of these books is much more vituperative, vengeful, and cruel than in earlier decades."[4] Russo's comic touch manages to dilute most elements of cruelty or vengefulness into gentle humor, but *Straight Man* does offer plenty of digs at the pretentiousness and self-importance of faculty members mired in the petty politics of university life.

Upon its release in 1997, *Straight Man* was widely and positively reviewed; the *New York Times* reviewer Tom De Haven commented admiringly that it was "the funniest serious novel I have read since—well, maybe since 'Portnoy's Complaint.'" De Haven continued, "The novel's greatest pleasures derive not from any blazing impatience to see what happens next, but from pitch-perfect dialogue, persuasive characterization and a rich progression of scenes, most of them crackling with an impudent, screwball energy reminiscent of Howard Hawks's movies."[5] *Publishers Weekly* concurred, observing that "Russo concocts an inspired send-up of academia's infighting and petty intrigues that ranks with the best of David Lodge, as we follow Hank's progress from perverse mockery to insight and acceptance. Readers who do not laugh uncontrollably during this raucous, witty, and touching work are seriously impaired."[6] Ron Charles, writing in the *Christian Science Monitor,* was just one of many reviewers to comment on Russo's talents for writing dialogue, noting, "Russo writes repartee that crackles with wit but never slides into artifice. Though his characters are often struggling against deep-seated sadness, the force of his wit is enough to convince us that such pain and sadness are not inevitable or final."[7]

Understandably most reviewers treated *Straight Man* simply as a success-ful addition to the small but flourishing subgenre of campus novels, often connecting Russo's characters and storytelling to those of David Lodge, Philip Roth, Kingsley Amis, Jane Smiley, and other writers who have tackled the complex and often absurd world of academia. A few reviewers, however, interpreted *Straight Man* as a novel that was less about campus politics and more about human nature. For example, Rita Jacobs, writing for *World Literature Today,* commented, "Richard Russo's work is more than merely 'an academic novel,' meaning it is not limited by a fusty formula. Nor is it a genre novel which focuses on an exploration of undergraduate peccadilloes, a kind of borderline bordello novel. Rather, Russo's fourth novel . . . is a complex, witty, and moving portrait of a very intelligent, middle-aged man trapped in a variety of ways."[8] Similarly a critic for the *National Catholic Reporter* argued that *Straight Man* transcends typical campus novels because Russo "uses the chaos of an academic department under budgetary pressure from without and lacking a core of integrity within to represent the larger chaos we know as the contemporary world."[9]

Such reviewers seem to have channeled Russo's own feelings about the nature and heart of *Straight Man.* Despite its solid credentials as an academic novel, Russo has maintained that the novel "really isn't about academia; it's about what happens to a man who's nearing 50, who has been, in a limited way, quite successful." Although Hank has achieved many of his life's goals, including marrying the woman he loves, raising two daughters, and building a house, he comes to realize that his novel from twenty years before "was responsible for his being promoted into the trap he's in now. Most of what is of consequence in his life is beginning to drain away."[10] Indeed, Hank's upcoming fiftieth birthday casts a long shadow over *Straight Man.* More than once Hank comments on his own appearance, sometimes congratulat-ing himself on his grace and long-leggedness but also acknowledging how much he has physically changed since arriving in Railton in his late twenties. Looking at the author's photo on the jacket of his one published novel, Hank thinks, "The bearded, shaggy-haired author who stares down the camera so piercingly from the jacket of *Off the Road* no longer greatly resembles the clean-shaven, thinning-haired, proboscis-punctured full professor who reflected back at me earlier from my kitchen window" (27). Hank later acknowledges to himself sadly, "I have all the classic symptoms of age . . . sleeplessness, creaking bones, inflexibility (physical and other)" (107), and he struggles to accept even the more minor consequences of aging (such as being moved from his "spiritual" position of outfielder on his recreational softball team to first base, where speed matters less). The major consequences of aging, including health problems such as his malfunctioning bladder, weigh even more heavily on him. Hank spends much of the novel suffering from a frustrating and painful inability to urinate, and despite his doctor's denials, he remains convinced that he has developed a kidney stone. Hank's frequent need to pee and his unsatisfying dripping become a running gag throughout a novel preoccupied with the many complications of growing older.

The story opens with Hank serving as the interim chair of his fractured English department while a doomed search to hire an outside chair drags on. The importance of tenure in the novel is not whether Hank will achieve it, as he has been tenured for many years, but rather the psychological effect of actually having tenure. For readers less familiar with the hiring policies of colleges and universities, tenure is a system established to protect the academic freedom of individuals who teach potentially controversial material. After an apprenticeship lasting approximately six years, assistant professors are evaluated by their peers and supervisors in a tenure review. Those who are denied their bid for tenure are customarily allowed to keep their jobs for one year and then are dismissed from the college or university. (This is what happens to Sully's son, Peter, in *Nobody's Fool*.) A professor who is awarded tenure is essentially guaranteed a lifetime of job security unless unusually serious circumstances prevail, such as criminal behavior on the part of the individual or dramatic budget cuts on the part of the institution.

Straight Man presents just such an unusual circumstance: West Central Pennsylvania State University is faced with such dire financial cutbacks that even tenured faculty are in imminent danger of being laid off—an almost unheard-of situation and one that panics Hank's irascible and only modestly talented colleagues. Rumors circulate that department chairs have been asked to generate a list of their faculty members who may be considered "expendable," and seniority or tenured status may not be used as a deciding factor. As acting chair, Hank is in the unforeseen and unenviable position of possibly having to create such a list, although he denies the existence of such a mandate until the end of the novel, when in fact the villainous campus

CEO, humorously named Dickie Pope, does in fact ask Hank to do just that. Hank, who has repeatedly promised his wife, his friends, and his colleagues that he would never accede to such a demand, is forced to consider the consequences of sticking to his guns. Making a list would keep Hank from losing his job; declining to do so would give the list-making power to any one of his many aggrieved colleagues who would be happy to see him fired.

Even before we know where the story is taking place or virtually anything about the characters' situations, we know that our first-person narrator, Hank Devereaux, has tenure. In the first scene of the first chapter, when Hank is suffering from an as-yet-unexplained nosebleed and his friend and colleague Teddy Barnes is driving him home, we learn not only that the two professors are tenured at their university but also that with that tenure comes, at least for Hank, a dissatisfying sense of inevitability, a belief that everything will work out. But the price of such security is a disappointing lack of drama in his life. As Teddy's aging Honda struggles to ascend a steep hill, Hank thinks to himself, "Teddy is sure we'll make it, and so am I. We have tenure, the two of us" (6).

Tenure remains a defining element of Hank's experience throughout the novel, primarily because achieving this professional status has robbed his life of any sense of unpredictability, and he realizes that, up until this round of draconian budget cuts, whatever trouble he was able to stir up in his corner of the university would not likely result in any serious repercussions. As he approaches his fiftieth birthday, Hank feels increasingly restless and dissatisfied with his life, which, while comfortable and gratifying enough, also has become a monotonous trap. Arriving in Railton twenty years earlier as the author of a successful novel, he believed that his position at West Central Pennsylvania University would simply be a brief stepping-stone on the path to a much more accomplished career. Hank's father, William Henry Devereaux Sr., was a famous scholar (the "Father of American Literary Theory" [xvii]), the author of multiple books and recipient of many prestigious positions at far more prominent universities. Hank's professional path has been much shorter and straighter. On the strength of his first and only book, he secured tenure and promotion to full professor, ruefully noting that "promotion in an institution like West Central Pennsylvania University was a little bit like being proclaimed the winner of a shit-eating contest" (27). Two decades later and still at the same small university, Hank yearns for some kind of excitement in his life; to this end he relentlessly goads his colleagues to distraction. He fantasizes about his wife having affairs, not because he wishes it were so or even thinks it likely to happen, but because it would disrupt the placid serenity of his life. He indulges in feeling "half in love" with several women on campus, including his secretary, a lesbian colleague in women's studies, and the daughter of a colleague who also teaches in Hank's department. He even enjoys (in a way) the possibility of being required to make a list of "expendable" colleagues and of perhaps being fired, wondering to himself, "What I'm really at a loss to explain is the odd thrill I feel at the possibility that the rumor [about the purge] might be true" (55). Even the possibility of a serious medical condition elicits more excitement than dread; after learning from his doctor that he has a rectal asymmetry that could indicate a tumor, Hank muses, "How to describe the strange exhilaration at this information? Fear? Surely. But more than this, and it's the 'more' that I can't explain" (252). In short, Hank longs for anything—even cancer—that would stir up his life and provide some respite from the relentless tedium of a mediocre career at a mediocre university.

When it comes to these longed-for disruptions of the same old routine, Russo clearly delivers. *Straight Man* takes place over the course of less than a week, plus an epilogue that, in grand nineteenth-century novelistic style, leaps ahead about four months to explain how everything turns out. But the five days of the actual novel are crammed with life-altering and perspective-changing events. Hank becomes a campus pariah and a national celebrity for threatening on the local news to kill "a duck a day until I get my budget" (118), endures an awkward and somewhat illicit hot-tub encounter, survives a recall vote by his department that would have stripped him of his position, is jailed overnight for drunk driving, suffers a medical emergency that lands him in the hospital, contends with the return of his famous father (now incapacitated and abandoned by the last in a series of graduate student trophy wives and mistresses), copes with the collapse of his daughter's marriage, loses his job despite the failed recall against him, receives his irascible father-in-law into his home for an extended visit, and buries his beloved dog, Occam.[11] Throughout it all Hank reflects on the meaning of his life and the absurdities that seem so prevalent within it.

Russo quickly establishes Hank Devereaux as a deeply flawed protagonist and a full-fledged comic antihero; self-involved and at times deliberately perverse, he seems to embody few traditional heroic qualities. In fact the first page of the novel reveals, through Hank's first-person narration, that not only is he "not an easy man" but also that he is almost universally found to be "exasperating" (xi). His penchant for infuriating those around him manifests clearly in the first chapter, which relates his painful recent encounter with Gracie DuBois, a fellow member of Hank's department. Hank relentlessly torments Gracie until, in her frustration, she inadvertently stabs him in the nostril with the uncoiled wire from her spiral-bound notebook. Over the course of the novel, Hank continues to provoke his colleagues and superiors, enjoying his ability to get a rise out of them every time. His roguish behavior and unwillingness to take seriously virtually any of the things his colleagues value culminate in their decision to vote on a recall of the chair, a scene made particularly memorable by Hank's awkward eavesdropping from the crawl space over the conference room.

Hank specializes in being a gadfly, goading his colleagues into open hostility with his straight-man routine. Russo provides a wide and entertaining cast of foolish, petty, pretentious, and academically inauspicious colleagues for Hank to target. But despite his coworkers' many obvious shortcomings, Hank's motivation for antagonizing them is not always completely clear, even to himself. Heading into the fateful department meeting where he is gigged in the nose, for example, Hank recalls, "I had not intended to belittle Gracie. At least not until I got started, after which it felt like the natural thing to do, though I no longer remember why" (21). A lack of clear motivation, however, does little to impede Hank's vexing behaviors, finally driving his friend Jacob Rose to claim, "You are the physical embodiment of the perversity principle" (361). Hank repeatedly insults Finny Coomb, an arrogantly incompetent instructor remembered for his two weeks of flamboyant transvestitism when he went off his meds, and openly mocks Campbell Wheemer, who teaches sit-coms instead of books and who corrects any use of the masculine pronoun by adding "or she," which quickly earns him the nickname "Orshee." Hank's provocateur tendencies do not end with his colleagues; he also writes satiric op-ed pieces for the Railton newspaper, under the heading "The Soul of the University," that offer "deadpan accounts of academic lunacy" (14). These pieces draw accusations that Hank "lack[s] high seriousness" and "undermin[es] what little support there is in the general population for higher education" (14–15). Russo seems to suggest that Hank's perverse need to antagonize his coworkers, in person and in print, indicates his own growing belief that the university, in fact, has no soul worth defending. In a place where mediocrity rules; departments are generally "silly, small, mean-spirited, [and] lame" (61); decisions are made by tyrannical, hypocritical dictators such as Dickie Pope; and a highlight of the semester is a faculty-administration donkey basketball game, there is simply no reason to take things too seriously.

Despite their lack of talent and (often) dignity, Hank's colleagues nevertheless take themselves quite seriously as academics, and Hank never misses an opportunity to comment on what he sees as character weaknesses of academics in general. In the first scene of the novel, when Teddy cannot figure out how to get his car's seat to slide back, Hank equates "academic"

with "helpless" (3). Later, in imagining the result of an imagined affair between Teddy and Hank's wife, Lily, Hank envisions that Teddy would "go
out and buy a gun and shoot himself in the foot by way of comic penance,
and then apologize all over again for lacking the courage to make a stronger
statement. He's an academic, after all, like the rest of us" (22). After Teddy
congratulates Hank for making his wild threat about killing ducks until he
receives his budget, Hank comments, "Like most academics, [Teddy] is fascinated by childish, unprofessional conduct" (123). When rumors circulate
about Hank's supposed list of expendable faculty, he notes wryly, "My colleagues are academics. They indulge paranoid fantasies for the same reason
dogs lick their own testicles" (204). What keeps Hank's steady disparage-
ment of academics from being especially vicious or cruel is that he seldom
fails to include himself in these condemnations. For example, in the final
scene of the epilogue, so many professors cram themselves into a small room
that they cannot easily exit. Hank observes that all they need to do is collectively step backward, away from the inward-swinging door, and concludes
that "a group of plumbers, a group of bricklayers, a group of hookers, a
group of chimpanzees would have figured this out. But the room contained,
unfortunately, a group of academics, and we couldn't quite believe what had
happened to us" (391). This sheepish inclusion of himself in the "us"—the
academics who are so easily bewildered by simple reality—allows readers to
perceive Hank as endearing (if also exasperating) rather than simply unkind
or ungenerous to his colleagues.

Hank lands in the position of interim department chair for the perverse
reason that his "lack of administrative skill is legend." His deeply divided
department votes for him because, as Hank recounts, "No one for an instant considered the possibility that I would do anything. No one imagined
I could locate the necessary forms to do anything. I am regarded throughout
the university as a militant procedural incompetent" (66). Hank has the last
laugh, as usual, because his colleagues have failed to take into account his
competent secretary, Rachel, who understands the paperwork and is quite
fond of her boss, who generously and effectively mentors her efforts at fiction writing. With Rachel's help, Hank proves that "a great deal of havoc
can be wrought in two semesters by anyone so inclined, at least if that person
is sufficiently insensitive to ridicule, personal invective, and threat" (67).
What Hank does not openly acknowledge, though, is that despite his claims
to have no political acumen, he is in fact extremely savvy when it comes
to understanding subtext, rhetorical strategies, and complex motivations.
Rather than being a renegade outsider unaware of "the details of political
machination" (66), he is actually a true insider to this world that he professes

to loathe, and he understands much more than his colleagues think he does. For example, when Hank is called into Dickie Pope's office after his television appearance threatening to kill a duck a day, he easily analyzes all of Dickie's rhetorical moves against him. Dickie begins, "'Lawyers and cops. Cops and lawyers. And I thought I was going to be an educator,' he moans theatrically, studying me as he does so. Surely this is a calculated tactic. I'm from the English department, and he's probably concluded I don't have much use for cops and lawyers. So, for the moment, neither does Dickie. Having established a common value system, maybe we can be friends. Maybe even do business" (158). Perhaps Hank's political acumen comes from being raised by academic parents, or perhaps it evolves as a function of his work as a fiction writer fascinated by characters and their motivations. But whatever the source, all of Hank's claims of administrative ineptitude are entirely disingenuous. He is much more of an insider in the lunatic world of academic politics than he cares to admit, even to himself.

  Straight Man, widely considered Russo's funniest novel, employs many kinds of humor. Most of his works have strong comedic elements that are largely based on unexpected situations or funny dialogue, and like *The Risk Pool, Nobody's Fool, Empire Falls,* and *That Old Cape Magic, Straight Man* fits perfectly into this category. Dialogue is perhaps Russo's greatest strength as a novelist; his ability to set up witty banter among Hank and his colleagues, his inventive use of malapropisms to showcase Mr. Purdy's dedication to Hank's imperious mother, and his hilarious portrayal of Lily's father earnestly explaining how he landed in jail for *not* shooting an "exceptionally tall, impolite, confused, deaf, big Negro" (370) who was collecting paper-route money showcase his ear for language and his considerable comic timing. Unlike most of his other novels (with the important exception of *That Old Cape Magic*), though, *Straight Man* also provides a steady stream of physical—even slapstick—comedy. The novel opens with Hank's gruesomely punctured nostril—a painful injury, to be sure, but an undignified and ridiculous one as well. Gags involving Hank's nose continue with the false nose and glasses he wears for his lunatic interview on television, which suggest that he is merely a caricature of a deranged professor (although too many witnesses—including members of the local PETA chapter—seem unable to get the joke). Several other scenes also incorporate physical comedy, including ones in which Hank urinates in his pants, Hank climbs into the ceiling and becomes trapped in the crawl space above the department conference room, Occam the dog uses his long pointy nose to "groin" Hank's guests, and all the academics become "trapped" in a small room.

More so than in his other novels, Russo also employs the technique of the running gag to buoy the comic effect of *Straight Man*. For example, Hank suffers throughout most of the novel with what he self-diagnoses as a kidney stone that blocks his ureter and makes it nearly impossible to relieve himself. The critic Eric Leuschner sees Hank as part of a pattern of "damaged professors" whose "bodily defect or medical malady [functions] as a primary character trait." But unlike academic characters who suffer and die from such serious diseases as cancer (as in Margaret Edson's *W;t* [1999]) or AIDS (as in Saul Bellow's *Ravelstein* [2000]), Hank endures a non-life-threatening urinary ailment that is magnified "in grotesque, comedic ways"[12] throughout the novel. Hank frequently contends with his aching inability to pee, and several scenes incorporate his musings as he drips miserably into urinals, onto bushes, and against trees in impotent frustration. Although his malady lacks dignity, it is at the same time full of symbolic importance; it intensifies as Hank struggles to cope with increasingly challenging situations—budget cuts, his father's return, his daughter's marriage crisis—and climaxes when he is offered the chance to become the next dean of arts and sciences. At this moment Hank, in intense physical agony, answers Jacob Rose's abstract philosophical question "What . . . the fuck . . . do you . . . *want?*" with the literal, visceral answer, "to *pee*" (362). Hank is finally able to release his pent-up urine (and then promptly passes out and lands himself in the hospital) only when he realizes that he must reject this professional opportunity and step away from the tenure system that has stultified his life.

Although *Straight Man* is full of unpredictable situations, the comedic elements arise largely from Hank's internal monologues, which reveal just how Hank manages to process the world around him. Russo's insights as a former college professor drive the plotlines of budget cuts and departmental bickering but also inform the ways Hank wrestles with the changes that seem to be sweeping through his workplace as well as his family. "The only kind of comedy that I'm interested in," Russo explains, "is comedy that's deeply rooted in character, in who these people really are, which seems to me to be a function of close understanding."[13] His understanding of the university environment and his sympathetic portrayal of a middle-aged man reckoning with a midlife crisis combine to create a portrait that is simultaneously comic and poignant.

Part of the way that Hank reckons with his own midlife crisis is by repeatedly returning to the story of William Cherry, a Railton man who had recently retired with his full benefits and a pension. One night Cherry inexplicably lay down on the railroad tracks and was decapitated by an oncoming train. His suicide mystifies his neighbors, who explain to news journalists that he had no reason to kill himself since "he had it made." The incident gnaws at Hank's mind, and as he tries to imagine Cherry's mental state, he wonders if, like him, "William Cherry also feared things would work out if he didn't do something drastic to prevent them" (5). That Hank perceives everything working out as reason enough to kill oneself helps to explain his seemingly perverse inclination to disrupt harmony and stir up controversy at all costs. Hank also feels that his chosen professional path—the same one as his emotionally distant, lecherous, opportunistic father—puts him in grave danger of coming to resemble his father in other ways as well. His wife Lily maintains that he should make his peace with who he is instead of trying so hard to distance himself from his father (281). But Hank steadfastly resists this pressure; like Sully in *Nobody's Fool,* he feels no great compulsion to renegotiate his feelings toward his father. Nevertheless it becomes clear that part of Hank's entire modus operandi is to define himself in opposition to his father; he makes his decisions based on what his father would not have done. As a result he becomes a long-term member of a single university and a subpar literary scholar but a relatively engaged husband and father.

Hank purports to subscribe to the philosophical notion of Occam's razor, which suggests that when multiple explanations exist, the simplest one is most likely to be true. His preoccupation with this concept of simple explanations surfaces repeatedly in the course of the narrative and even extends to include naming his dog Occam. Hank comments early in the novel, "Were it not for Occam's Razor, which always demands simplicity, I'd be tempted to believe that human beings are more influenced by distant causes than immediate ones. This would be especially true of overeducated people, who are capable of thinking past the immediate, of becoming obsessed by the remote" (28). Despite his apparent allegiance to simple explanations, however, as one of these overeducated people who can become obsessed by the remote, Hank lives much of his life in direct violation of Occam's dictates. For example, his fractured relationship with his father, revealed primarily through flashbacks and narrative asides, continues to haunt Hank's daily life. Dealing with the residual pain from his father's abandonment leads Hank to admit to Lily that engaging in self-deception and pretense is worth the effort to maintain the "costly illusion that I am not what my father is" (281), certainly a violation of Occam's principle. The critic Richard Costa claimed, "For Hank Devereaux, invoking Occam's urge to simplify becomes a check on any tendency to self-indulgence. Its implications are profound, but application is difficult."[14] Indeed, although Hank consistently seeks the simplest explanation for any given situation, he has trouble implementing this theory.

Instead he resorts to his own version of the perversity principle, unnecessarily complicating matters with his insistence on infuriating and undermining practically everyone around him.

Humor helps to define *Straight Man*, but it is certainly not the only force at work in this novel. Russo uses a comic narrator to tell a serious story that, at bottom, is less about university life and more about a family on the brink of significant change. Hank's father returning (albeit briefly) to his life, his daughter's marriage in tatters, his university's impending faculty purge, and his own awkward reckoning with his fiftieth birthday collectively force Hank to acknowledge, first to himself and then to others, how much he truly cares about them. Russo reveals this emotional work partly through the form his novel takes. *Straight Man* begins with the burial of Hank's boyhood dog, Red, described in the first chapter,[15] and ends with the interment of another, his beloved Occam, accidentally run over by Finny. Russo draws significant parallels between this cycle that starts with Hank's first dog and ends with his last; as Hank buries Occam and realizes how much he resembles his father, who, forty years before, too had ruined his shoes and blistered his hands on a borrowed shovel as he dug Red's grave, he acknowledges to himself, "*I had tried to be unlike him, but look at me*" (384). In addition, although Hank's last encounter with Hank Devereaux Sr. takes place only in his imagination, it becomes clear that Hank has finally achieved some emotional peace regarding his father. He recognizes how much his father has influenced his life, but instead of indulging in reconciliation or false regret, Hank clings firmly to his belief that in the most important ways, he and his father are different. So Hank powers up his final thought to the vision of his father watching him: "*Well, I didn't have to go borrow a shovel, old man*" (384).

The epilogue to *Straight Man* takes readers forward in time, from April to August, and reveals some of the long-term fallout from the week-long crisis detailed in the rest of the novel. As a result of the university "purge," Orshee has been fired, Hank's alcoholic friend and colleague, Billy Quigley, has been reassigned, and Finny has been offered the chance to finish his dissertation at the University of Pennsylvania and, barring that, rejoin the faculty as an instructor. Jacob Rose is now the CEO of the university, and Hank's longtime nemesis, Paul Roarke, is the dean of liberal arts. Hank has accepted a new role at the university, giving up his tenure and dividing his time between university and high school teaching. Janice Rossen notes, "It is no accident that many of the best University novels are about someone leaving academe at the end of the book"[16]; while Hank may not have left academia entirely, he has certainly renegotiated his role in it. Although the epilogue does dance dangerously close to an unambiguously happy ending (including even a literal list of things that contribute to Hank's happiness, among which are his health, his marriage, his friends, his finances, and, oddly, his father's death, which makes Hank feel that he is "my own man at last" [382]), there is also a sense that such happiness could be fleeting. As one reviewer astutely observed, "For Richard Russo's small-town Americans, contentment is always understood as a temporary state, just as exuberant high spirits are recognized as a thin, but useful, disguise for sorrow."[17]

CHAPTER 6

Empire Falls

When Richard Russo's fans ask him how much of what he portrays in his books is actually true, he replies, "All of it. But some of it, I made up."[1] In the case of *Empire Falls* (2001), his fifth novel and the winner of the 2002 Pulitzer Prize for fiction, the author certainly draws on truths from his own childhood in Gloversville, New York; his experiences living in Waterville, a small Maine town not unlike the fictional Empire Falls; and parenting two daughters who were teenagers when their father was writing this novel. The parts that Russo "made up"—the details, histories, and daily lives of the Robys, the Whitings, and the other families who live and work in Empire Falls—converge to tell a story that includes several elements familiar to readers of other Russo novels. The major characters in *Empire Falls* are regular people working regular jobs, seeking happiness within the boundaries of their dilapidated mill town, and trying to come to terms with being abandoned by the industries that once supported the local economy. About his penchant for blue-collar, "everyman" characters, Russo explains, "I've always been interested in ordinary people swept up in economic and political forces they can't begin to comprehend, as well as in the changing face of American labor. Becoming a writer has only deepened my sympathies for working people, who are always, it seems to me, the first to be sold out."[2] So, like *Mohawk*, *The Risk Pool*, and *Nobody's Fool*, *Empire Falls* explores the lives of everyday people struggling to eke out livings and maintain some hope for their futures in a town darkened by boarded-up factories and limited opportunity.

Empire Falls is an expansive novel—not as long as *Bridge of Sighs* but with a larger cast of characters. It primarily follows the Roby family, long-time residents of Empire Falls, Maine, through three generations. Miles

Roby, the forty-two-year-old manager of the Empire Grill and the protagonist of the novel, is separated from his wife, Janine, who has taken up with
the obnoxious owner of a local fitness club. Their daughter, Tick, is a bright
high school sophomore struggling to deal with her parents' separation as well
as the heartbreaking challenges of trying to fit in with the high school social
scene. Miles's father, Max, an amiable layabout who periodically abandoned
the family during Miles's youth, schemes relentlessly for the cash he needs
to get to Key West, Florida, where, he maintains, he can drink beer and
enjoy the company of women who appreciate him. Miles's brother David,
whose arm was badly injured in a car accident, helps him run the diner, and
Charlene, the waitress whom Miles has loved (unrequitedly) since he was
a teenager, waits tables. An inherently decent and goodhearted man, Miles
struggles to overcome his inertia and to cope with the guilt he still feels for
betraying his late mother's deepest wish: for him to leave Empire Falls behind
and start a new life.

At the same time, the novel details the history of the town of Empire
Falls and its wealthy ruling family, the Whitings. Francine Whiting, the rapa-
cious widow of C. B. Whiting and the owner of nearly everything in Empire
Falls worth owning, runs the town like a manipulative bully. She lives by
the motto "power and control" and has long exerted a mysterious interest
in and control over the Roby family, particularly Miles's late mother, Grace.
The novel gradually reveals that this enigmatic connection stems from a brief
love affair between C. B. Whiting and Grace Roby, which Francine knows
about but Miles does not until late in the novel.

Empire Falls is bookended by a prologue and an epilogue, written in italics and intended to convey elements of the story that fall beyond the present.
Other chapters, interspersed within the narrative and also italicized, further
expand the segments of the story that occur in flashback, encompassing
sequences from Miles's childhood or even before. The prologue begins by
explaining the history of the patrician Whitings, the richest family in Empire
Falls, and the marriage pattern of the Whiting men, who "invariably gravi-
tated, like moths to a flame, toward the one woman in the world who would
regard making them utterly miserable as her life's noble endeavor" (14). It
also details C. B. Whiting's temporarily successful efforts to change the flow
of the Knox River, which persisted in depositing trash and dead animals upon
the bank near his house, by dynamiting a piece of land upstream. Rivers, both
literal and figurative, feature prominently in the novel and more than once are
used as metaphors to illustrate the inexorable paths our lives take. As Francine Whiting lectures Miles later in the novel, "Lives are rivers. We imagine

we can direct their paths, though in the end there's but one destination, and we end up being true to ourselves only because we have no choice" (163). This metaphor takes on literal meaning in the final scene of the novel as Mrs. Whiting is swept away by the river during a flash flood.

The title of the novel *Empire Falls* obviously derives from the name of the town, but it also resonates with the narrative's larger theme of widespread personal and community dissolution. Russo noted in a 2005 interview that the title is a complete sentence and is meant to describe "the various empires that we seem to be on the downside of in some way or another: the downfall of the Whiting empire as it's been sold off to the multinationals, which is the story of a lot of mill towns in the United States; the declining influence of faith in our daily lives or the difficulty of trying to place where that faith should be; the family in decline."[3] After the factory layoffs and outsourcing of manufacturing jobs, towns such as Empire Falls are left lying in their own rubble; as storefronts empty and bulldozers turn formerly bustling city blocks into parking lots that remain largely unoccupied, residents are left only with the dark joke about plentiful parking in downtown Empire Falls. Waning numbers of parishioners in the town's two Catholic churches prompt the sell-off of one church and the merging of the two congregations. In addition the power of the family unit in *Empire Falls* is sorely tested; indeed one child is so badly abused by his family that his uncontainable pain flows back violently into the community. As the empires of capitalism, religion, and family disintegrate all around them, the residents of Empire Falls are left wondering, what comes next?

Empire Falls is the first and, to date, only Russo novel set in Maine, a state where he has lived, at least part-time, since the early 1990s.[4] But like many of his other blue-collar novels, the setting is simultaneously specific and vague; Empire Falls is a down-on-its-luck town based on the real-life central Maine towns of Skowhegan and Waterville, but it could just as easily be conceived as a mill town in New York or Pennsylvania or West Virginia or anywhere else jobs have been lost to outsourced manufacturing and the people have been left behind. Part of the universality of the setting stems from Russo's decision not to include overt representations of Maine dialect or many references to specific Maine locales. Rather he focuses on the relationships between people, their connections to their work, and their struggles to create opportunity in circumscribed conditions. When readers have commented that Russo succeeds in representing the particularities of Maine culture, he has responded, "No, I don't think I got Maine right, I think I got class right. I think I got mill towns right. I think I got the kind of work that people do and the kinds of problems that they have as a result from the kind of work that they do. I got that right, but I've been watching that my whole life, not just in Maine."[5]

Another element of the appeal of *Empire Falls* stems from its focus on an American experience largely outside the mainstream. Blue-collar workers living out their lives in the same failing mill town where they were born do not tend to make headlines. Russo acknowledges that his books are "odes to a nation that even I sometimes think may not exist anymore except in my memory and my imagination," but he adds that ignoring most of current American popular culture allows him to write more imaginative novels and that writing about the real American experience would mostly yield stories about "a lot of people sitting in front of television sets."[6] Instead he endeavors to focus on larger questions of socioeconomic class, the nature and rewards of work, and the age-old quest for love, all couched within a comic novelist's sensibilities.

Empire Falls incorporates many narrative elements that have, over time, come to be closely associated with Richard Russo. While not nearly as funny as his 1997 novel, the satiric *Straight Man, Empire Falls* does include many examples of Russo's trademark humor, from Miles's and Tick's literate hobby of identifying "Empire Moments"—unintentionally funny signs around town ("No Trespassing Without Permission")—to the more gentle observational humor that characterizes Miles's narrative. Max Roby, perhaps the funniest character in the book and reminiscent of Sam Hall from *The Risk Pool* and Sully from *Nobody's Fool,* proves immune to social expectations of hygiene, manners, or respect for private property. His relentless efforts to pinch a twenty-dollar bill off Miles, for example, and his indifference to all manner of food stuck in his beard help create a character so entertaining and yet exasperating that it becomes nearly impossible to hold against him the misery he caused his wife. At other times humorous descriptions of such things as the operation of Mrs. Roderigue's utter sham of an art classroom also serve to lift the veil on a more unfortunate element of the story, in this case the staggering incompetence of a teacher. Russo sees no cognitive dissonance in such a portrayal, noting, "I want that which is hilarious and that which is heartbreaking to occupy the same territory in the book because I think they very often occupy the same territory in life, much as we try to separate them."[7]

Another familiar trope in Russo's fiction is the diner that anchors both the town and the story; like the Mohawk Diner in *The Risk Pool* and Hattie's Lunch in *Nobody's Fool,* the Empire Grill is the physical heart of the novel. Horace Weymouth and Walt Comeau play daily games of gin rummy at the counter, Tick's high school crowd cycles in and out of the booths, and Charlene scoops up tips and dispenses advice with the efficiency that comes with long years of practice. The Empire Grill is an important, if informal, community center; it provides its working-class patrons a gathering place where they can discuss the latest rumors about Massachusetts investors contemplating buying the mill, debate the prospects of the high school football team this season, and speculate on Francine Whiting's latest machination. Although it has a long history in Empire Falls and is the only non-fast-food restaurant that remains in town, it struggles amid an essentially empty downtown business district and is prevented from becoming profitable by Mrs. Whiting's stubborn unwillingness to procure a liquor license. Miles's brother, David, manages to make some headway by opening the restaurant for dinner three nights a week and by developing innovative international menu themes to attract the local college crowd. The diner also serves as a site to explore elements of socioeconomic disparity; the narrator notes that out-of-town students and faculty who visit the Empire Grill for Chinese night or Mexican night "would consider the grill's worn-out, cigarette-burned countertop and wobbly booths 'honest' or 'retro' or some damn thing" (102), implying that such a perspective requires significant economic distance. To outsiders, the Empire Grill is a sort of relic from the past, whereas it is nothing of the sort to longtime residents. Nevertheless the Robys manage to co-opt this notion and work it to their advantage—one of the few advantages they can muster while the restaurant struggles under Mrs. Whiting's subversive ownership.

Beyond the diner, the deserted downtown storefronts, the boarded-up factory, and the other physical manifestations of life in a down-at-the-heels manufacturing town, *Empire Falls* returns to more intangible themes that run through the heart of Russo's body of work. One of these themes is the apparent impossibility of enjoying a successful, happy married life. Although Russo has repeatedly explained that his own marriage of more than four decades is both solid and satisfying, marriages in his fiction seldom share the same fate. *Empire Falls* is no exception. Francine Whiting, whose marriage to C. B. ended with his suicide, cynically observes, "Most people . . . marry the wrong person for all the wrong reasons. For reasons so absurd they can't even remember what they were a few short months after they've pledged themselves forever" (169). Her pronouncement seems to apply to virtually every marriage in the novel, all of which fail for one reason or another. More extreme examples of marital disharmony include the long line of Whiting marriages, which seem invariably to include attempted murder or suicide, but other marriages inevitably seem to fail as well, if not for such violent reasons. In some cases, though, the character who initially seems most responsible for the marital breakdown appears less culpable as more information is revealed. For example, Grace and Max Roby seem incompatible from the very start, and his general unreliability and irresponsible tendencies make it appear as if he is wholly to blame for his steady, devout wife's unhappiness. However, readers eventually learn of her affair with C. B. Whiting and must accept that Grace shares some responsibility for her marital undoing. Similarly, Miles's ex-wife, Janine, is initially presented as selfish and vain; her voracious and widely broadcast sexual appetite for the ridiculous Walt Comeau makes her appear equally ridiculous. But gradually we learn that Janine has long yearned for genuine connection in her life, not just through sex but also through meaningful communication, and the stubbornly uncommunicative Miles has unwittingly been stifling her for years. Russo not only demonstrates the old axiom about every story having two sides but also shows compassion for those characters who appear to be the cause of another's unhappiness but in fact are suffering too.

Empire Falls yields few glimpses of romantic bliss, and the dynamics of most relationships in the novel seem to suggest that happiness, or perhaps something like peace, might be more profitably sought elsewhere. One of those places is the church, and Russo unself-consciously demonstrates the strong emotional hold that Catholicism has on Miles. One of the larger themes of the novel considers the role of faith in people's lives and the consequences of discounting the power of the church to provide stability and community in a fragmented and unpredictable world. As in *The Risk Pool, Empire Falls* responds to this question in part by presenting a benevolent priest who provides some stability for the main character. As an altar boy raised in the church by a devout mother, Miles feels a lifelong connection to Roman Catholicism and attends mass almost every week. One of his closest friends is Father Mark, a young closeted gay priest with whom Miles finds much-needed comfort, fellowship, and understanding. Miles's willingness to paint the peeling facade of the church for free, even as he struggles to balance the demands of his job and family, suggests his determination to offer something back to the church that has sustained him for a lifetime.

However, the role of Catholicism in the novel is not always so benevolent, and Russo certainly does not portray the priests as less flawed than anyone else in town. Indeed, Father Mark, with his guilty sexual longings, and Father Tom, with his aggressive dementia, combine to offer a problematic vision of a church unable to minister effectively to its parishioners. Whatever gravitas the elderly Father Tom may have had in his younger years is now long gone; he has recently betrayed the confidentiality of the confessional by revealing to Miles that his then-wife was having an affair with Walt, after

Janine went to confession in the hopes of absolving herself of sin while at the same time cagily entrusting her secret to a priest with Alzheimer's. Years earlier Father Tom rewarded Grace Roby's constant faith with merciless cruelty when she came to him to confess her adulterous affair with C. B. Whiting. Instead of showing compassion, he demanded that her penance include a personal apology to C. B.'s widow, Francine. The ramifications of this act have transcended any traditional form of penance, as Francine has put into motion a long, slow revenge. She first ensnares Grace in the Whitings' lives by hiring her as a personal assistant and caretaker for her disabled daughter. Later she thwarts Grace's dream for Miles to leave Empire Falls by luring him back and saddling him with the Empire Grill, a situation he never wanted but cannot seem to escape. The power of the church, Russo implies, runs deep in communities such as Empire Falls and yet seems to cause at least as many problems as it solves. Although Miles maintains his commitment to Catholicism throughout the novel, the title of Father Mark's sermon, "When God Retreats," seems a more fitting summary of the role of faith in *Empire Falls*. Miles, however, displays a level of forbearance and equanimity, even in the face of truly exasperating circumstances, that perhaps demonstrates a truly Christian way to live in the world. In the midst of a cultural crisis of faith, Miles shows self-sacrifice, tolerance, and acceptance of forces he cannot completely understand, and through these traits Russo may be revealing a vision for a kind of Christian humility separate from the notion of organized religion.

Russo returns to third-person omniscient narration in *Empire Falls*, closely following Miles's thoughts but also allowing readers into the minds of certain other characters. The narrative point of view keeps us close to Tick's perspective, and even Janine and Max reveal their inner lives through the omniscience of Russo's narrative voice. A few characters, though, are entirely closed off from this omniscient narration and thus remain permanently unknowable to readers. Francine Whiting, for example, has many conversations with Miles, but the narration includes only his thoughts, not hers. This narrative distance underscores the unpredictable nature of her decisions and observations, and it propels the enigmatic nature of her involvement with the Roby family. Some of the Whiting family history, however, is revealed in the italicized flashback chapters, and readers are able to piece together, slowly, the motivations behind Francine's velvet-gloved malevolence toward the Robys. An even greater mystery, though, is the character of John Voss, whose thoughts are never shared with readers and whose backstory is told only in fragmented, secondhand bits, through Otto Meyer's impressions as he reviews John's social-work file and Horace Weymouth's experience watching John abuse his dog. Although readers learn of the extreme abuse and neglect he suffered at the hands of his drug-dealer parents and witness the cruelty he experiences at the hands of his fellow students (particularly Zack Minty), John's character remains entirely inscrutable. Even after John shoots and kills a classmate, a teacher, and the principal and leaves another girl permanently disabled, Russo offers no omniscient voice to explain John's actions or to foster readers' empathy. Like real-life survivors of a mass shooting, readers are left only with questions about what could have prevented such a heartbreaking tragedy.

The inclusion of a tragic school shooting in *Empire Falls* was, in part, born out of the cultural context in which it was written. Russo began composing the novel not long after a rash of school shootings erupted in the 1990s, including the massacre in West Paducah, Kentucky, in 1997. Two years later when the Columbine High School shootings occurred in Colorado, Russo was deeply immersed in the manuscript. He included a school shooting in *Empire Falls,* he says, because after Columbine, when the question of *why* was on everyone's lips, he realized that "the answers that are typically offered to such questions are sociological and political—tighter gun control, return to family values, reducing violence on television and video games. Better answers to such impossible questions, I've always thought, are offered by novels, which ask you to live horror rather than simply witness or think about it."[8] Fiction can explore tragic incidents imaginatively and try to explain why they occur in ways that journalism never can. Russo's experience wrestling with school shootings was deepened by his perspective as a father of two daughters, and he has confessed that he, like Miles, feels that he can never be vigilant enough when it comes to a child's safety and that there are some things that one simply cannot prevent from happening. "Such knowledge," Russo explained, "is the basis for parental night sweats, and I've come to think of this book in exactly those terms—one long, vivid, parental night sweat."[9]

The other side of the "parental night sweat" coin is the fact that *Empire Falls* was conceived, in part, as a "father-daughter love story."[10] Russo's fiction up to this point had largely been concerned with fathers and sons; although the relationship between Anne Younger and her father occupies a central place in *Mohawk* and Hank Devereaux's daughters contribute an important layer of family complexity to *Straight Man,* Russo's primary fictional relationships are mostly male. *Empire Falls,* which was started when Russo's two daughters were both teenagers, was spawned in part from his overwhelming love for his girls, coupled with his fear and anxiety about the kind of world they were about to enter. "I was quite confident about them and the kind of young women that they were," he recalled in a 2002 interview, "but I was a little bit worried about what the world had in store for them."[11] These worries were no doubt stoked by the stories of everyday high school cruelties that he encouraged his daughters to share with him. His younger daughter, Kate, got especially "mixed up in both the creative process and in my own head with the character of Tick that I knew I was going to have to take to a nightmare place."[12] Russo recognizes his debt to Kate in a special note in the acknowledgments, thanking her "for reminding me by means of concrete detail just how horrible high school can be, and how lucky we all are to escape more or less intact."

Russo's loving paternal instincts clearly surface in the character of Miles Roby, who is undoubtedly the most attentive, selfless, generous father in all of Russo's novels. As the protagonist of *Empire Falls*, Miles fits easily among the series of Russo characters who are well-intentioned, small-town, working-class men who have never strayed from their hometowns for long. Dallas Younger in *Mohawk*, Sam Hall in *The Risk Pool*, Sully in *Nobody's Fool*, and Lucy Lynch in *Bridge of Sighs* all reveal different personalities and priorities, but they are quintessential Russo heroes because, as Russo has explained, "they're not terribly dramatic people necessarily or successful in the ways that we like to measure success, and yet [I] see in their everyday lives a kind of heroism."[13] They work hard at thankless, often low-paying, dead-end jobs and suffer the insecurities of lives built on a fluctuating economy, a surplus of workers, and a general lack of jobs. Miles proves to be a dedicated worker, but his tragic flaw is his passivity; as a *New York Times* reviewer described, "He can't say no to C. B.'s widow (who rules Empire Falls like the Yankee transplantation of a Tennessee Williams matriarch), can't save his ex-wife from another unhappy marriage, can't rein in his cantankerous father, can't protect the 16-year-old daughter he adores—can't, in short, do anything at all."[14] The tangle of obligations he feels toward nearly everyone in his life, including his late mother, effectively paralyzes him. Francine Whiting diagnoses him as suffering from an "overdeveloped sense of responsibility" (164), but Russo has attributed Miles's stasis to the fact that he feels overpoweringly trapped—"by the past, by his faith, by an old love, by his devotion to his daughter, by his own decency." Miles's available options are far from clear; Russo went on to comment, "I'm always drawn to the character whose dilemma is such that I can't imagine what I would do if I were in his shoes."[15]

Miles's mother, Grace, imagines that the answer to her son's problems—perhaps to problems in general—is to leave Empire Falls far, far behind. Grace dreams of his departure starting the day she returns from her fateful

Vineyard dalliance with C. B. Whiting—she establishes right then that for
Miles, college, preferably a faraway college, is nothing less than mandatory—
and Mrs. Whiting's summoning of Miles back to Empire Falls when Grace is
dying of cancer causes her to suffer an excruciatingly hard death. But *Empire
Falls* is far from the only novel to weigh the options between leaving town
and staying put. In fact in many of Russo's other novels, those who struggle
to make ends meet in battered little towns dream of lives in other places, but
through a lack of imagination, education, or opportunity, they seldom succeed at leaving their hometowns behind. A handful, however, do manage to
get away: Anne Younger relocates to the sunny Southwest in *Mohawk;* Ned
Hall builds a new life for himself in New York City in *The Risk Pool;* Bobby
Marconi trades Thomaston for Venice in *Bridge of Sighs*. However, most of
Russo's characters end up exactly where they started. In *Empire Falls,* Miles
dreams of relocating to Martha's Vineyard and opening a bookshop there,
and he and Tick do find respite on that island after the trauma of the school
shooting. But Miles falls into the category of those who "almost get away,"
and inevitably, it seems, he is drawn back to Empire Falls. His ultimate
resumption of life there seems to imply that life's most meaningful changes
are not connected to one's geographic location. By the end of the novel,
the usually inert Miles has been inspired to act. He defies Francine Whiting
by throwing his lot in with David and Bea as they renovate Callahan's; he
fistfights Jimmy Minty; he rescues Tick from the high school massacre and
puts her on the road to recovery. He proves to himself that he is capable of
action, and this, for him, means more than changing addresses or following
his mother's dream of living in Martha's Vineyard. He may never be "Mr.
Empire Falls" (294), as Jimmy Minty brags of being, but he learns to find
grace in those aspects of his life tied not to geography but rather to the bonds
of love, loyalty, and friendship.

Although *Empire Falls* beat Jonathan Franzen's popular *Corrections*
for the 2002 Pulitzer Prize for fiction, the novel was not universally well
received, and it was not short-listed for any other major fiction awards.
Reviewers' responses varied widely, and clearly some of them remained
more impressed with Russo's earlier novels, especially *The Risk Pool* and
Nobody's Fool, than with *Empire Falls*. For example, the reviewer for the
Economist opened his lukewarm review with these comments: "Richard
Russo's sweeping prologue to *Empire Falls* is so good that readers are likely
to flip through the rest of the novel wondering what went wrong. Disap-
pointingly, Mr. Russo returns to the same lunch counter banter in the same
knock-off of Gloversville, the run-down town in upstate New York where
he was raised, that fills out three of his four previous novels. As ever, flawed

but endearingly eccentric regular folks quaff weak coffee and wonder if the mill's gonna sell."[16]

Most reviewers, however, embraced *Empire Falls* more enthusiastically; Janet Maslin asserted in the *New York Times* that "this is easily Mr. Russo's most seductive book thus far,"[17] and the reviewer for *Library Journal* described *Empire Falls* as "a sensitive, endearingly oddball portrait of small-town life, a wonderful story that should appeal to a wide audience."[18] *Empire Falls* was even included on the *Harvard Business Review*'s list of the "Best Business Books of 2001" because of its revelation that "businesspeople are complex mortals, driven far more by relationships and emotionally charged memories than by profits."[19] The critic A. O. Scott pinpointed both the complexity and the appeal of *Empire Falls* in his observation that "the people of Empire Falls are not held down simply by fate or by their own bad choices but by the active collaboration of their neighbors and loved ones: the cruel priest who helps break Grace Roby's spirit, the myopic art teacher who tries to break Tick's, and the teenage football star (Jimmy Minty's son Zack) who mocks and torments a lonely misfit named John Voss." Scott continued, "One of the old-fashioned pleasures of 'Empire Falls' comes from the delicious expectation that the villains will receive their comeuppance and that the good guys will find at least a morsel of the satisfaction they so desperately (and often half-consciously) crave."[20]

Once again Russo delivers on readers' wishes for appropriate distribution of rewards and punishments. At the end of *Empire Falls,* as is the case with most of Russo's novels, unsettled plot details are satisfactorily resolved, and a short epilogue reveals the answer to one lingering question: why C. B. Whiting and Grace Roby never ran away together. The epilogue also describes how Francine Whiting's corpse was washed away in a flood (with Tommy the demonic cat clinging to it, thus completing the grotesque image), firmly establishing that Mrs. Whiting will no longer pose a problem for Miles or for the other residents of Empire Falls. Indeed, Empire Falls appears to be on the upswing at the end of the story; Massachusetts financiers have indeed decided to invest in the town, and the renovation of the textile mill to house a brewpub and corporate offices has begun. In addition Miles, upon his return from Martha's Vineyard with Tick, finds himself a partner in the new Callahan's restaurant, so it seems that the Robys' immediate financial future is somewhat secure. Still at issue, though, are the socioeconomic consequences of such an economic revitalization of the town. The creation of new jobs and opportunities is, of course, a positive change, but Miles recognizes that "the lion's share of the wealth generated would never reach the citizens of Empire Falls. The houses they couldn't afford to sell last year would be houses they couldn't afford to buy the next" (462). Investments from a credit-card company can keep a town like Empire Falls afloat, but it is the Whiting families of the world, not the Roby families, who stand to benefit the most. Yuppified restoration and a service-oriented economy will exploit the townspeople just as the mill owners had done a generation before, and such short-term solutions cannot address the larger socioeconomic problems rooted in an America divorced from its manufacturing roots. Nevertheless, Russo manages to find unexpected salvation for the working-class community of Empire Falls, too often nostalgically relegated to some notion of a bygone America, by situating it within a new economic order that is very much part of the nation's future.

Empire Falls had barely appeared on bookshelves when Paul Newman contacted Russo and suggested himself for the movie role of Max Roby. With Newman's encouragement, Russo was convinced to adapt the novel himself to fit HBO's requirements for a three-and-one-half-hour, two-part miniseries. The film, directed by Fred Schipisi, aired on HBO in 2005 and featured an all-star ensemble cast, including Newman as Max, Ed Harris as Miles, Helen Hunt as Janine, Philip Seymour Hoffman as C. B. Whiting, Joanne Woodward as Francine Whiting, Robin Wright Penn as Grace, and Danielle Panabaker as Tick. The film was warmly received; it was nominated for nearly thirty awards and won seven, including two Golden Globe awards (one for best miniseries or motion picture made for television and one for Paul Newman for best performance by an actor in a supporting role in a miniseries or motion picture made for television) and one Primetime Emmy award (Paul Newman, for outstanding supporting actor in a miniseries or a movie).

CHAPTER 7

Bridge of Sighs

"It generally takes me four or five years to write a novel; this one took longer," explained Richard Russo in a 2007 interview, shortly after his sixth and longest novel to date, *Bridge of Sighs,* was released. "I spent six years, every day, with Lucy and Sarah and Noonan and the other characters in *Bridge.* Love is not too strong a word for the relationships that developed."[1] The love that flourished between the author and his characters spills over into the plot, as the primary tension of the novel takes the form of a love triangle, of sorts, that emerges among the three main characters in high school and lasts throughout their adult lives. As is perhaps to be expected from "the bard of Main Street U.S.A.,"[2] the story is set against a backdrop of a decaying Rust Belt town defined by its defunct tannery and the trail of cancer diagnoses left in its wake. One of the three main characters escapes his small-town life and his abusive father, but the other two spend the rest of their lives in their broken-down town, building a life together that is not defined by its circumscription but rather proves to be both rich and satisfying, if occasionally bittersweet. In fact the novel as a whole, as one reviewer put it, can be read as "a love letter to the lost art of staying put."[3]

Bridge of Sighs tells the story of sixty-year-old Lou C. Lynch (who gets saddled with the unfortunate and persistent nickname "Lucy" in kindergarten) over the course of more than fifty years of his life. About half of the chapters are told from his first-person perspective, as he tries to write a memoir that recounts his childhood and also serves as a history of his hometown of Thomaston, New York. The other chapters are told in omniscient third person and are divided between Sarah, Lucy's childhood sweetheart and wife of forty years, and Robert Noonan, a famous painter living in Venice, Italy, who when he was a boy lived in Thomaston, went by the name Bobby

Marconi, and was Lucy and Sarah's best friend, their "third musketeer from senior year of high school" (6). Lucy and Bobby first come to know each other as children; from the beginning Lucy's infatuation—even obsession—with Bobby colors much of his childhood and adolescence. Sarah also becomes infatuated with Bobby (even though she is Lucy's girlfriend), and he falls in love with her as well. But circumstances intervene; when Bobby is eighteen, he brutally beats his father, with whom he has had a long and troubled relationship, and a warrant is issued for his arrest. Bobby changes his name to Robert Noonan and flees to Canada, never to return to Thomaston, and his love for Sarah (and hers for him) remains forever unspoken. Lucy and Sarah marry, raise a family in Thomaston, and inherit the convenience store once owned by Lucy's parents. As the years pass, Lucy remains preoccupied with Bobby and their lost friendship; as the novel opens, Lucy and Sarah are planning a trip to Italy during which they hope to reunite with Bobby for the first time in more than four decades. Much of the novel is told in flashback, through Lucy's supposed memoir, and it focuses on the childhood and adolescence of these three friends, their families, and their experiences up until their senior year of high school, when a series of decisions made in an instant set the course for the rest of their lives.

On the surface Russo's own life seems to resemble more closely that of Bobby Marconi than Lucy Lynch's; Bobby leaves Thomaston after high school graduation, changes his name, and finds his way to a new life as a painter in Venice. Russo left the tannery town of Gloversville at the age of eighteen and, except for a few summers while he was still in college, seldom returned. In fact, however, he has claimed to identify just as closely with Lucy as with Bobby; Russo explained, "I am the boy who left and I am the boy who stayed. And the dichotomy of that has made me think even more and more pointedly about the place."[4] As Lucy confesses in his memoir, "I can't help thinking that somehow Bobby actually managed to do what we all imagine we might back when we're young, before time and repetition erode and render mundane the mystery of existence. Bobby alone, it seems to me, invented both a life and a self to live it" (157). Much of the novel focuses on the concept of inventing a self, of choosing what life to live, instead of passively inheriting a set of circumstances and living within them.

For the settings in *Bridge of Sighs,* Russo maps two primary locations. Part of the novel is set in Venice, home of the real Bridge of Sighs, a city that Russo loves and to which he returns in his 2013 novella, *Nate in Venice.* Robert Noonan settles there and establishes his reputation as an internationally acclaimed painter; most of the chapters focusing on his adult life take place in that city. But the majority of the novel transpires in the fictional town

of Thomaston, a crumbling upstate New York community that strongly resembles the fictional Mohawk featured in Russo's first two novels, which in
turn is modeled on his own real-life hometown of Gloversville, New York.
Thomaston's lifeblood had long been the tannery, which employed much of
the town's citizenry before it closed down, even as it poisoned the Cayoga
Stream and triggered numerous cases of cancer among the residents unlucky
enough to live along its banks.

The class orientation of his characters in *Bridge of Sighs* takes center
Thomaston is divided geographically into three distinct areas, each of
them corresponding directly to the socioeconomic class of its residents. The
West End is where the poorest citizens reside, and one neighborhood in the
West End, called the Hill, houses the town's small African American population. The East End is home to Thomaston's working-class, aspirational,
somewhat economically mobile families. These two large neighborhoods,
implausibly yet literally separated from one another by "Division Street,"
are economically eclipsed by the Borough, where the small moneyed class
lives. The Lynch family starts its life in Thomaston in a shabby apartment in
the West End, shortly before Lucy enrolls in kindergarten. The family then
moves up in the world, to a modest, single-family home in the East End, after
Lucy suffers the first of what turns out to be a lifelong series of cataleptic
spells. As an adult he purchases a home in the Borough, where he lives in the
present of the story. The Marconi family also proves to be socially mobile,
at least within the confines of Thomaston's limited economy. The Marconis
begin alongside the Lynches on Berman Court in the West End, then move
to the East End when Mr. Marconi lands a full-time route at the post office,
before finally settling in the Borough. These migrations from the poorest to
the finest neighborhoods in town offer the narrator frequent opportunities
to describe and muse about these discrete locations, and they perhaps give
rise to the oft-repeated notion that Russo is an author primarily concerned
with place. Although he vividly portrays different neighborhoods with intense geographical detail reminiscent of Sinclair Lewis's *Babbitt* (1922), these
areas of town serve chiefly as socioeconomic class markers, and it is these
class markers that have largely preoccupied Russo throughout his career. In
a 2007 interview on National Public Radio, in which he discussed *Bridge
of Sighs,* Russo tried once again to assuage his reputation as a place-based,
or regional, writer, asserting, "People confuse class and place. I don't write
about place really. I write about class."[5]

The class orientation of his characters in *Bridge of Sighs* takes center
stage; when Lucy is still a boy, his mother, Tessa, tries to describe to him the
limits of class mobility, especially in Thomaston. The African Americans, she
explains to her bewildered son, would likely remain in the Hill neighborhood

no matter how hard they worked, and the wealthy Borough residents would probably stay in the Borough. Lucy recalls this conversation in his memoir, remembering how she exposed to him the hard truth about class divisions: "In America . . . the very luckiest were insulated against failure, just as it was the unavoidable destiny of the luckless to remain thwarted" (65). Of their own family's fortunate relocation from the West End to the East End, Tessa reminded her son, it was just luck. People like them, who were in the middle, sometimes had the chance to climb up in the world, but they could also slip back down. As a child Lucy understood that identities in Thomaston were closely tied to street addresses, and even Lucy's kindly father, Big Lou, felt bound to explain to his son that even though "this is America . . . [and you] got a right to go wherever you want" (97), sometimes it is better to stay in your own neighborhood and not upset people. As an adult, Lucy believes that one of his greatest achievements is his ability to transcend these boundaries, both geographical and social, that divide other Thomaston residents. Although he lives in the Borough, he owns retail and residential property in both the East End and the West End, walks daily through the different neighborhoods, and considers himself "spread all over town" (13). He remains friendly throughout his life with Gabriel Mock Junior, an African American, and even begins the process of adopting an abandoned African American child; yet Lucy's individual egalitarianism does little to break down the formidable barriers of class and race that comprise Thomaston's inflexible social foundation.

Bridge of Sighs is deeply engaged in questions about how family and class determine one's fate, questions that Russo previously raised in *Empire Falls, Nobody's Fool,* and *The Risk Pool.* In a 2007 interview, he commented about *Bridge of Sighs,* "One of the larger themes of this new novel is destiny: What determines who we become, the shapes our lives take?"[6] Socioeconomic class contributes to this, of course, and individual ambition, but *Bridge of Sighs* particularly emphasizes the notion that important moments in childhood forever change the trajectory of one's life and can come to define one's adult experiences. These unanticipated moments repeatedly emerge as powerful harbingers of the future. Lucy's whole life takes a sharp turn, for example, the moment the kindergarten teacher reads his name incorrectly on the first day of school. Years later he recalls, "Miss Vincent's roll sheet contained her students' first names, their middle initials, and, of course, their surnames. If that's what she'd read that first morning—Louis C. Lynch—I suspect I'd have had a different childhood" (9). Instead the name "Lucy" takes hold among his classmates and dogs him throughout his childhood.

In another childhood moment that proves to have lasting consequences, Lucy is abducted by Jerzy Quinn and his gang of elementary school bullies after school one day, marched through the woods to their "clubhouse," and deposited inside a trunk. The boys try to scare Lucy even more by pretending to saw through the trunk while he is inside, but the tables turn when Lucy slips into the first of his cataleptic spells and the boys, unable to rouse him, fear they have actually scared him to death. This initial spell prompts Lucy's parents to borrow money from Tessa's family and move out of the West End, in the hope of removing their son from his tormentors and giving him a fresh start. The location of the Lynches' new house, right across from Ikey Lubin's store, later gives Big Lou the idea to buy the place after he is laid off from the dairy, which later leads to his acquisition of additional stores. Thus the entire "Lynch Empire," in a way, can be traced back to that unexpected childhood moment when Lucy was forced into a trunk by Jerzy Quinn and his gang.

Other unanticipated moments too prove to have dramatic and lasting repercussions. In an episode from his youth that Lucy has effectively suppressed for years, he reveals his high school friendship with a lonely boy named David, who twice made awkward homosexual advances toward him. After David kissed him for the second time in two days, Lucy "shoved David away and told him I didn't want to be friends anymore" (561). The next day David hanged himself in his garage. In a less lethal but just as lasting departure, Nan Beverly is spirited away from Thomaston by her parents the day after she and Bobby had sex for the first time—an encounter that Bobby had long anticipated but that ended up happening only in response to Nan's anger at her parents and desire to do something spontaneous and reckless to hurt them. Unconfirmed rumors circulate that pregnancy prompted Nan's sudden departure, but pregnant or not, her permanent disappearance from Thomaston results from a single instance of bad judgment. In another unanticipated moment, one of bravery, Gabriel Mock the Third screws up the courage to defy racial norms and ask Sarah Berg to the movies when they are both fourteen years old, prompting Perry Kozlowski to beat him so viciously that he never fully recovers and is able only to limp through to adulthood, where death in Vietnam awaits him.

Russo admits that *Bridge of Sighs* was the most difficult of all his books to write, partly because it is the darkest of all his novels but also because he made a "terrible mistake right at the start" as he tried to sort out his narrative perspective. As it turns out, he had made this mistake before. When he was writing *Nobody's Fool,* Russo originally thought that Sully could carry the whole book through his first-person narration, and only after writing hundreds of pages did he realize that the book required a more omniscient approach. Similarly, Russo began writing *Bridge of Sighs* completely in Lucy's voice. In a 2010 interview Russo described how, after drafting about 250 pages of the manuscript, "I felt trapped inside Lucy's voice, because he's not a reliable narrator. He doesn't know the truth of the story he's telling." So Russo switched perspectives and began telling the story again, this time from Robert Noonan's point of view. After 250 more pages, he had managed to establish that both men were in love with the same woman, but he felt that something was still missing: Sarah's voice. Russo recalled, "How fair is it to have them both in love with the same woman—who would see things differently than both of them? You have to give her a say." So he embarked on a third section, from Sarah's point of view, and quickly realized that he had essentially written three separate novels, and none of them had an ending. He sent the enormous, unwieldy, seven-hundred-page unfinished draft to his agent, Nat Sobel, who recognized that the book needed to be completely restructured. The novel would hold together if Russo could pull off a sort of "juggling act, going back and forth, past and present, narrator to narrator." In the end, Russo explained, "Everything about that book ended up in a different place, almost, than where it was originally. I will always think of Nat as saving that novel, because I really was at a loss. I was completely up a stump. I didn't know what happened next or how to go about it."[7]

The end result is a novel very different from Russo's other works, despite the similarity of location and the revisiting of several themes common to his novels. *Bridge of Sighs,* his least comic novel by far, reckons more overtly with despair than any of his other works. Lucy's childhood is indelibly marked by his experience of being trapped in a trunk by the local bullies, and while he does manage to escape that trunk, as an adult he creates traps for himself that are just as devastating. Lucy develops a lifelong habit of seeing what he wants to see and repressing what he cannot process. He represses his memories of his friendship with David to the point that, a few years later when asked about him in school, Lucy simply cannot remember the boy at all. When Lucy catches a glimpse of Sarah's sketch of Bobby, drawn during Sarah's summertime visit to her mother's Long Island home and clearly presented as a symbol of her love for him, Lucy recalls, "I knew immediately what it meant, but in a heartbeat I'd hidden both the drawing and its significance away where it would trouble me no further. I think I've remembered it no more than half a dozen times in all the years since" (466). Most important of all, Lucy sabotages Sarah's attempts to contact Bobby in Italy, afraid that if the two of them should reunite, she will fall in love with Bobby all over again. Lucy's anxiety and guilt about this decision seem to climax in that moment when he slips into a cataleptic spell and imagines himself crossing halfway over the Bridge of Sighs in Sarah's painting and almost does not return from that shadowy place. Russo noted of that moment, "That's as dark a place as I've ever been in a book. [Lucy's] suffering is so intense there."[8] No levity exists to alleviate the pain of Lucy's journey; no witty one-liner can take away the anguish and guilt of betraying a loved one.

Some of Russo's favorite themes emerge in *Bridge of Sighs,* perhaps most notably the importance and complexity of father-son relationships. Bobby Marconi's difficult relationship with his abusive father is of a piece with several other father-son pairs in Russo's oeuvre, although this one ends with a particularly violent beating and the son's lifelong estrangement from his hometown. The animosity between them recalls the deep hatred that Sully feels for his father in *Nobody's Fool,* a hatred that Sully nurtures throughout his adult life. Mr. Marconi is a more complex character than Big Jim Sullivan, but he nevertheless falls on the broad spectrum of paternal incompetence that also includes, among others, Dallas Younger, Sam Hall, Sully, Miles Roby, William Henry Devereaux Sr., and William Griffin.

Lou Lynch, or "Big Lou," is an altogether different sort of father and the only one in Russo's novels who is loved so deeply and unequivocally by his son. Big Lou, who seems hopelessly unsophisticated and naive to the other adults in the novel—especially his quick-thinking and sharp-witted wife Tessa—seems to Lucy to be the very model of how a person should think and act. Lucy defends his father, emulates him, even celebrates his physical resemblance to him, for Big Lou is the only person who seems to love Lucy unconditionally and can create for him a haven of safety and protection in what Tessa calls "a mean old world" (563). Lucy's growth over the course of the novel in large part stems from his eventual and reluctant willingness to achieve some critical distance from his father, to see him more objectively and less through the lens of indiscriminating hero worship. Lucy does reach this level of maturity and comes to understand that for Big Lou, "the world wasn't a complicated place. Its rules mostly made sense and they were for our own good. I've always wanted to be the person he believed me to be, which at times has kept me from being a better one. A terrible realization, this" (563).

Russo also revisits the tremendous damage that the leather manufacturing industry has wrought on both the environment and the health of its workers, a theme that surfaces first in *Mohawk* (1986) and continues through *The Risk Pool* (1988), "Poison" (collected in *The Whore's Child and Other Stories* [2002]), and *Elsewhere* (2012). In Thomaston cancer rates are unnaturally high; Ikey Lubin, the original owner of the corner store, dies of cancer, as does Big Lou. Sarah contracts breast cancer and has a mastectomy;

at one point Robert Noonan believes that his medical symptoms suggest cancer, a diagnosis which, given his hometown, does not surprise him. As in other novels, the tannery owners in *Bridge of Sighs* reap tremendous profits while poisoning waterways and then leave town for Florida or Atlanta or other warm places; as Tessa says to Big Lou, who believes the tannery owners would never close the shops and bankrupt the town, "*They'll* get out clean. *They* aren't stupid" (238). Of course the tanneries do close, and many in Thomaston are thrown out of work, just as in the fictional town of Mohawk and the real town of Gloversville. But Lucy echoes the voice of Mather Grouse in *Mohawk,* and Russo's own grandfather in *Elsewhere,* when he writes that "it's worth remembering that this same tannery sustained our lives for more than a century, that the very dyes that had caused the Cayoga to run red every fourth or fifth day also put bread and meat on our tables. When I was a boy, people were afraid only when the stream *didn't* change color, because that meant layoffs and hard times would soon follow" (11). This frightening conclusion that Lucy presents at the beginning of the novel, "that what provides for us is the very thing that poisons us" (11), not only applies to the tanneries but also helps readers to understand his complicated relationships with his father and with his friend Bobby—relationships that both sustain and harm him throughout his life.

Although quick to note the lack of comic elements in the novel, reviewers of *Bridge of Sighs* both recognized and embraced the presence of the many working-class elements that have come to define Russo's novels. For example, a reviewer for *Booklist* raved that *Bridge of Sighs* "gives full expression to the themes that have always been at the heart of [Russo's] work: the all-important bond between fathers and sons, the economic desperation of small-town businesses, and the lifelong feuds and friendships that are a hallmark of small-town life."[9] Another reviewer praised the novel's complexity and scope, noting, "Nobody now writing rivals Russo at untangling the knots of family connection, love and sexuality, ambition and compromise, fidelity and betrayal that link and afflict a formidable gallery of vividly observed, generously portrayed characters."[10] In addition Russo, who has been accused from time to time of shortchanging his women characters, garnered this compliment: "One of Russo's strengths is writing about fathers and sons, but in *Bridge of Sighs,* his strongest characters are women. Louis's mother and wife are the saddest but wisest people in Thomaston."[11]

Many reviewers seem united in the criticism that the weakest element in *Bridge of Sighs* is Russo's portrayal of his African American characters, particularly Gabriel Mock Junior and his son, Gabriel Mock the Third, also called Three Mock. Some reviewers have suggested that the black characters never manage to transcend stereotypes and speak embarrassingly like stock characters.[12] Others indicated that the Mock family feels artificially inserted into the story to add an element of social conscience. The story line of the Mocks certainly does carry strong overtones of social injustices that extend across two generations. Gabriel Mock Junior had a crush on Tessa when both were children, and when he was eleven years old he kissed her in public and took a beating from his father because of it. As an adult, Mock landed the Sisyphean task of painting the fence around the crumbling Whitcombe Hall; it took a year to paint it, and by the time he got back to where he started, it was time to start again. When Lucy was a teenager, Gabriel's son, Three Mock, was savagely beaten by Perry Kozlowski for escorting a young Sarah Berg to the movies; the boy barely recovered and hardly ever spoke afterward. For a time, though, he was shepherded around the high school by Sarah Berg's father, an English teacher, seemingly as a reminder to the youths of Thomaston about the beating that many of them witnessed but were too cowardly to stop. Three Mock later dies in Vietnam, and his father, who ultimately ends up working for Lucy as a building caretaker, never recovers from the trauma of losing his son. Overall few African American characters appear in Russo's novels; for the most part his literary landscapes incorporate far more diverse socioeconomic classes than racial differences, much like the rural northeastern towns upon which he bases his fictional settings.

African Americans do appear, however, in minor supporting roles throughout Russo's fiction; in *Nobody's Fool*, for example, Hattie's diner employs a black cook named Roof. In a few cases when such black characters appear in Russo's fiction, they are the victims of white-on-black violence. In *The Risk Pool*, Drew Littler goes to jail after battering a group of black youths outside a pool hall. In *Straight Man*, Hank's father-in-law lands in jail for threatening to shoot the brother of his black paperboy (but manages only to shoot down his own porch roof, which lands on both of them). Thomaston, however, is the only town in Russo's fiction acknowledged to have an actual black neighborhood, and with the possible exception of Wussy, Sam Hall's mixed-race friend in *The Risk Pool*, the African American characters in *Bridge of Sighs* occupy the most prominent roles of all Russo's black characters. Perhaps most unusual of these is Kayla, a more-or-less abandoned African American child whom Sarah meets on Long Island and brings home to Thomaston to raise. In some ways Kayla is defined less by her race, however, than by her tremendous need for love and her ability to connect with Sarah, who is experiencing grave doubts about her marriage and her life choices. Not all reviewers accepted this unlikely scenario; one noted pointedly that "the book's final sequence, in which Sarah travels to the Long Island home of her long-dead mother and winds up adopting a neglected black girl, feels as if it is imported from another novel altogether."[13] But Kayla is rendered as a believable character—flawed, needy, self-centered, and yet lovable.

In his review of *Bridge of Sighs* published in the *New Yorker,* Louis Menand drew an interesting connection between this novel and James Joyce's *Ulysses* (1922), noting that the three key characters in each novel share certain significant characteristics. Lucy Lynch, "the small-town entrepreneur, canny and naïve in equal parts, a plodder and a dreamer," evokes the character of Leopold Bloom. Sarah, "the clever and worldly wife to whom [Lucy] is blindly devoted," resembles Molly Bloom. Bobby Marconi, like Stephen Dedalus, is "the angry boy who flies by the nets, going into exile and becoming an artist." Menand went on to note that Russo "adapts, without attribution, a line from Joyce's novel (we are always 'moving through space, yes, but also through time, meeting ourselves'), and Lynch, just like Leopold Bloom, has lost a child."[14] In this model, then, Russo's Thomaston becomes like Joyce's Dublin, elevated from its modest position to become a subject worthy of literary examination. Just as Joyce fled Dublin in order to write about Dublin, Russo too understands that in order to write about people similar to the ones he grew up with in Gloversville, he must take advantage of both geographic and temporal distance from his hometown.

Invoking *Ulysses* and the story of Stephen Dedalus, however subtly, seems particularly appropriate in light of Russo's emphasis on creative expression in *Bridge of Sighs*. Writing, in the form of a memoir, becomes a vital creative act for Lucy, one that helps him achieve the psychological distance from his past that he needs in order to move forward. But painting ranks as especially significant in this novel, and the creation of art supplants words, in many cases, as a critical form of communication.

Bridge of Sighs is not Russo's first novel to use art as an important vehicle for self-expression; in *Empire Falls,* Tick Roby's artistic abilities help to define her character and create a connection between her and John Voss, a troubled youth who also displays some artistic talent. But in *Bridge of Sighs* art becomes a much more central theme. Sarah Berg's mother is a professional artist, and as a young woman Sarah too exhibits considerable ability. In fact the drawing she made of her brother who had died of leukemia is what first brings Lucy and Sarah together. The following day she presents Lucy with a drawing of his whole family at Ikey's, with Lucy and Sarah holding hands and Bobby Marconi walking in the door; this prophetic drawing represents the interpersonal dynamic for much of the rest of the novel. Sarah is indeed absorbed into the Lynch family, just as the picture shows, and Bobby remains on the threshold, always present in their lives and yet just outside the action.

It is also through her art that Sarah comes to realize her true feelings for Bobby, and the sketch she does of him during the summer before her senior year of high school reveals to her the love she feels for him but has resisted acknowledging to herself.

In the novel's present, art remains a primary theme. Bobby Marconi has transformed himself into Robert Noonan, an internationally famous painter whose lifelong hatred of his father seems to be ameliorated by the experience of drawing a young Sarah from memory. The light he paints in his portrait of Sarah bleeds over into the dark canvas of his father's portrait, allowing him to see his father differently and reach a moment of, if not forgiveness, at least something closer to peace. Sarah in the novel's present returns to her art and creates her own masterpiece, a rendition of the Bridge of Sighs in Venice, where prisoners on the way to their cells "came to understand that all hope was lost" (387). One reviewer suggested that this painting metaphorically transforms the railroad trestle under which Lucy was imprisoned in a trunk—the experience that caused the first of his cataleptic spells and came to define much of his childhood—into a thing of beauty. Lucy experiences the very last of his spells when he figuratively enters this painting and "finds the hope of a way out of his melancholy."[15]

Also through art the decades-old tension between Sarah and Bobby—their unspoken, unrecognized love—becomes resolved. Noonan's masterful painting of Sarah, *Young Woman at a Window*, was never meant for her to see, but through a series of tremendous coincidences, Sarah finds out about the art show just as she is passing through New York, and she decides to attend the opening. Seeing her younger self in that painting reveals to her the love that Bobby (now Noonan) had continued to feel for her all those years. In response to the painting, Sarah writes a letter that discloses just how close the two of them had come to living altogether different lives. She explains to him that the moment she found out about her mother's death, she sought out Bobby instead of Lucy. After waiting long enough "to feel like a bad person," she left Bobby's empty apartment and found comfort in the arms of Lucy and his family. At that moment she knew that she would spend her life with the Lynches at Ikey's, "where it was warm and safe and good" (619). Had circumstances been only slightly different, if Bobby had been at his apartment, perhaps the two of them would have ended up together. Ultimately, though, Noonan's act of painting Sarah and then her response to the secret that the painting reveals allow the two characters finally to acknowledge their deep feelings for one another. The experience is bittersweet, however, because the two never meet again, and Noonan dies that very evening of an aneurysm.

Lucy never learns of Sarah and Bobby's final encounter or how the creative act of painting led to their final understanding of one another. But Lucy experiences one final redemption through art, in the last chapter of the novel, when Sarah reveals a new drawing to complement the one she originally drew of his family in Ikey's. In the new version Lucy and Sarah replace Lou and Tessa, their son, Owen, fills the spot formerly occupied by Lou's brother, Dec, and Kayla appears on the threshold, where Bobby had once appeared. Lucy realizes that this new picture has the same purpose as the former one: "She drew us—her and me—together in that one, which was how I'd known we were. Now she's telling me that we're still together, that she's returned for good. . . . In my darkest hour I imagined myself lost in Sarah's Bridge of Sighs, and now she's given me a work of art I can truly live in" (636).

One reviewer commented about *Bridge of Sighs*, "It's the genius of Russo to show that nostalgia is not simply the roseate glow of a shared past that ropes the flawed, timid denizens of Tannery Row together. Nostalgia includes the pain, horror and nastiness of the past as well."[16] Russo sustains this nostalgic tone throughout the novel, in part through the use of Lucy's memoir as a way to record the past through his eyes. By viewing Lucy, Bobby, and Sarah as both adolescents and adults, seeing the consequences of the choices they made when they were so young, Russo forces us to wonder whether we are all stuck in some version of our own adolescence. What elements of our own lives can be traced directly back to who we were years ago? Are we always some iteration of our younger selves? Can we ever know for sure? *Bridge of Sighs* reminds us that even though the events of our youth seem indelibly marked upon our consciousness, we seldom remember those events the way they actually happened. Time and distance do their jobs; we repress some occurrences and magnify others in order to create a narrative that makes sense to us, one that we can live with. Russo reveals these truths gently, but that makes them no less painful. Despite its moments of joy and connection, the entire novel is suffused with a sense of loss that emanates not only from the absence of loved ones but also from the loss of the town itself. Once vibrant and prosperous, the tannery town is dying a slow death, and as Lucy meditates on all the elements of his past that his present no longer contains, he writes, "The loss of a place isn't really so different from the loss of a person. Both disappear without permission, leaving the self diminished, in need of testimony and evidence" (318–19). Despite the new beginning that comes with Kayla's adoption at the end of the novel, *Bridge of Sighs* focuses more on the experience of loss than any other of Russo's novels.

At the conclusion of *Bridge of Sighs,* most plot questions are resolved neatly, if not altogether happily. Robert Noonan dies, but not before making that final connection with Sarah that Lucy will never know about. Yet despite this secret that Sarah keeps to herself, her marriage to Lucy seems destined to endure. The addition of Kayla to their family gives them someone new to live for, and a reason for Lucy to look ahead to the future instead of back toward the past, as has long been his habit. Sarah forgives Lucy for his deceitful sabotage of their trip, and even more important, Lucy seems to have forgiven himself. Perhaps as a result of his psychological entering into Sarah's Bridge of Sighs painting, where he found himself tempted to let himself pass over into the darkness but was pulled back by the memory of his father, he sets aside his memoir project, content to enjoy the present instead. The final moments of the novel bring the reader back to the very beginning, with a new trip to Italy in the works. Russo commented to an interviewer about this circular structure, noting that when Lucy says at the beginning of the book that he and Sarah are going to Italy, "he's lying." Lucy knows they are not going to see Bobby, and he knows what happened to Sarah's letter and why Bobby has not written back. But the novel concludes with the line, "We will go," and, as Russo notes, "this time we believe him. Because that enormous journey he's taken is from one sentence to the same sentence. . . . He returns to his initial statement, except this time it's true. There's an element of human understanding in it, but I'm hoping that when that moment strikes the character, it hits us as readers not in the head, but in the heart."[17]

CHAPTER 8

That Old Cape Magic

That Old Cape Magic (2009), Russo's seventh novel, recounts the tragicomic story of Jack Griffin, a screenwriter and college professor, whose marriage nearly falls apart due to his inability to make peace with the memory of his difficult (although hilariously portrayed) parents. The novel is divided into two halves, each of which is anchored by a wedding scene. In part 1 Jack's daughter Laura's childhood friend gets married on Cape Cod; in part 2 Laura gets married on the coast of Maine. But Laura Griffin is decidedly a minor, albeit important, character. This novel chronicles the story of her parents—mostly her father—and his struggles to understand his relationship with his parents, his feelings for his wife, his ambivalence about his career, and his own faulty assumptions about how his life would actually turn out. As such, *That Old Cape Magic* revisits the familiar Russo theme of middle-aged men facing crises in their lives that force them to reevaluate their choices and priorities. At the same time, as one critic noted, "the novel comprises an exploration of how our parents' attitudes inevitably permeate our own, for better and for worse."[1]

The novel opens with Jack Griffin (or Griffin, as he is known) driving to Cape Cod, Massachusetts, to attend the first wedding of the novel. Cape Cod holds a powerful, almost magical hold over Griffin's imagination; the shore towns of the Cape are where he and his parents vacationed every summer of his childhood, driving from Indiana to a series of beach rentals of varying quality. Griffin's parents, both Yale-educated English professors, aspired to prestigious careers at an Ivy League school or some other esteemed northeastern college, but a stagnant job market yielded them only positions at a large state university in the "Mid-fucking-west" (6), as they bitterly called it. Their disappointing careers and acrimonious marriage, tainted by multiple affairs and general unhappiness, were leavened only by their annual pilgrimages to Cape Cod. "One glorious month, each summer," Griffin's mother described it. "Sun. Sand. Water. Gin. Followed by eleven months of misery" (7). As they crossed the bridge onto the Cape each summer, Griffin's parents would sing "That Old Cape Magic" to the tune of "That Old Black Magic," the 1942 song first popularized by Glenn Miller. Decades later Griffin's perceptions of not just Cape Cod but, in fact, all facets of his life remain colored by his parents' destructive cynicism.

In an effort to distance himself from his parents' values and vices, Griffin charts a very different career path for himself: Hollywood screenwriting. At first he revels in his parents' overt disapproval of his career, his lifestyle, and even his wife, Joy,[2] who does not have an advanced degree; upon learning of their engagement Griffin's mother asks snidely, "What sort of person doesn't do graduate work?" (31). But as a result of the plan that Griffin and Joy make while on their Cape Cod honeymoon, a plan he comes to think of as the "Great Truro Accord" (named after the town where they vacationed), Griffin eventually gives up screenwriting for college teaching (more in accord with his parents' careers), and the family leaves California for a big rambling house in the Connecticut countryside—the kind of house Joy has always dreamed of owning—a "professor's house" (46). In the story's present, the fifty-seven-year-old Griffin feels bewildered that his life so closely resembles his parents', despite all he did (or thought he did) to prevent this very outcome. Even harder, he must face the fact that the resemblances do not stop at surface-level similarities; he has deeply internalized his parents' cynicism and selfishness and has become, as Joy claims, "a congenitally unhappy man" (147). Hardest of all, he reluctantly comes to realize that despite his parents' many serious failings, he loves them anyway.

Much of the first half of the novel presents flashbacks of Griffin's life. He recounts the early years of his marriage and his struggles to adjust to being a member, at least through marriage, of Joy's close and loving, although occasionally exasperating, family. Compared to his parents, Joy's family seems to him like another species altogether—they want to play games, go golfing, and actually spend time in each other's company. Joy's parents, Harve and Jill, ask Griffin questions about his work because they are genuinely interested, and they encourage the young couple to visit more often. Griffin "didn't dislike them exactly" (47), but he finds his in-laws annoyingly bourgeois and conventionally minded, attracted to gated communities, golf, and Republican politics. To Griffin, his brothers-in-law, twins Jared and Jason, are ridiculous meatheads, and his sisters-in-law are shrieking drama queens with a maddeningly imperfect command of English. Griffin's goal is to distance himself and Joy from all of them as much as possible, and he finds it hard to imagine that his wife does not view her own family with the same combination of contempt and antipathy with which he views his own. His policy regarding their families is stunningly simple: "a plague on both their houses. Have as little to do with Harve and Jill, and with William and Mary, as decency permitted" (50). Throughout his married life, Griffin believes that he follows through on his end of this bargain; he refuses to "inflict" his parents on Joy, but his ability to keep his parents away physically does not prevent them from casting a long shadow over Griffin's life. His efforts to distance himself from his own parents blind him to the fact that Joy deeply loves her family and honestly enjoys their company. Griffin's and Joy's fundamental incompatibility regarding the appropriate role of extended family in their lives sows a seed of discontent that blooms later in the novel and very nearly destroys their marriage.

Part 1 of *That Old Cape Magic* contributes to readers' understanding of Griffin by presenting many details about his childhood experiences, his parents' fractured marriage, and his father's turbulent and apparently one-sided relationship with Claudia, his much younger graduate-student-turned-second-wife. The story of the Browning family also appears for the first time in part 1 and then resurfaces repeatedly throughout the rest of the novel. One summer on Cape Cod the lonely, twelve-year-old Griffin meets Peter Browning, a boy in a neighboring cottage, and they become fast friends. The Brownings essentially adopt Griffin for those two weeks of summer vacation, welcoming him into their family and including him in their cookouts and beach trips. The attractive Mrs. Browning becomes the object of Griffin's adolescent crush, and Mr. Browning takes the boys bodysurfing and gives them sparklers to play with at night. Taken together, this couple provides an idealized alternative to his own quarrelsome, neglectful parents, and Griffin remembers that "he'd fallen in love with the whole Browning family, and every day, even the rainy ones, was radiant" (60).[3] As an adult, Griffin attempts to write a story about his experiences that summer, "The Summer of the Brownings," but his early drafts fail to convey the intensity of his feelings for this family and instead seem to focus inadvertently on his own parents. As it turns out, Griffin cannot tell the story of the Brownings well until he recognizes the truth of his own story: Griffin has not entirely come to terms with the role his parents have played in his life. Over the course of *That Old Cape Magic*, he struggles to learn the truth behind his memories of that summer; ultimately he revises and publishes the story in a literary magazine, but the process of revisiting his experiences of that summer proves far more important to him than the story's ultimate publication.

Griffin also spends part 1 of *That Old Cape Magic* driving around with his late father's ashes in the trunk of his car, a clear symbol of his inability to reckon fully with his past. Ostensibly, Griffin's goal is to scatter these ashes somewhere on his father's beloved Cape Cod, but he finds himself unable to actually do so. At first he rationalizes that he needs to wait for Joy, who is arriving at the wedding in her own car, so she can serve as a lookout or at least witness Griffin's last words as he scatters the ashes. But it soon becomes clear that something other than a lack of a good jetty, a witness, or a lookout prevents him from parting with his father's remains. Although his halfhearted efforts to scatter the ashes provide some comic moments in the story, his ultimate reluctance to perform this final act for his father indicates the depth of Griffin's unresolved issues regarding his parents.

The first half of the novel culminates in Laura's friend Kelsey's wedding, after which Griffin and Joy appear to be on the brink of averting serious marital discord and returning to some level of stasis. Their recent falling-out led to their separate arrivals on the Cape, but the lovely wedding and their daughter Laura's happy announcement that she has become engaged to her boyfriend, Andy, combine to create for Griffin and Joy an evening of both sexual and psychological connection. Later that night, on the threshold of sleep, Griffin feels a "surge of almost painful affection" (121) for Joy and profound respect for Laura, who thoughtfully included her childhood friend Sunny Kim in the wedding festivities, even in the moments just following her own engagement. Griffin even feels uncharacteristically kindly toward his mother and makes plans to invite her to visit the Cape for a few days later in the summer. Part 1 ends on such a positive, hopeful note that there can be nowhere to go but down.

Sure enough, part 2 opens with this crushing summary: "How quickly it had all fallen apart. Even a year later, most of it spent in L.A., the speed of what happened after Kelsey's wedding took Griffin's breath away" (125). The morning after Kelsey's wedding, Griffin and Joy find themselves on a path heading almost certainly toward divorce. A quarrel about petty issues quickly escalates into a confession that Joy had, at one point, been in love with Griffin's longtime Hollywood screen-writing partner, Tommy. Griffin knew that Tommy had been in love with Joy for years, but he never suspected that Joy might reciprocate those feelings. This revelation prompts Griffin to recall the many times he had behaved badly toward Joy, cynically criticizing her parents, channeling his own parents' scathing contempt toward everything that mattered to her, making important decisions without her, trying to reconnect with his former Hollywood life without letting her know. In the end Griffin is "forced to entertain the possibility that he was in the wrong"

(142), but even at this point he is not willing to admit this possibility to Joy. In a rhetorical move designed to illustrate just how deeply estranged Griffin is from his own feelings, Russo casts the scene in which Joy and Griffin break up into a movie script, complete with stage directions and a dialogue labeled "HUSBAND" and "WIFE." In this heartbreaking conversation, Joy (as "WIFE") accuses Griffin of allowing his parents to poison their marriage specifically and his whole life in general, even though he thinks he is doing everything possible to shut them out. In response to the HUSBAND's denial that his parents intruded upon their married life, the WIFE counters, "I'm saying that out of sight isn't out of mind. You think you don't let your mother into your life—into *our* lives—but you blame *her* when a bird craps on you. Think about that. You believe your father's gone because he died, but he *isn't* gone. He's haunted you this whole year. Right now he's in the trunk of your car, and you can't bring yourself to scatter his ashes. Do you think maybe that *means* something?" (145–46). This insight is clearly obvious to Joy, and at this point to readers as well, but Griffin still cannot accept the idea that his parents function as anything but a cautionary tale to be applied, sparingly, to his own life. In his compulsion to deny this truth—that he remains profoundly connected to his parents—he allows his marriage to collapse. He takes a writing job with Tommy in Los Angeles and leaves Joy, his job, and their Connecticut home to return to the West Coast.

During the yearlong gap between the two parts of the novel, Griffin works, largely unsuccessfully, as a television screenwriter in Hollywood and spends several stretches of time with his mother in Indiana during the last months of her life. In the present of part 2 Griffin heads to Maine for the second of the novel's two weddings, this one his daughter Laura's. On this trip he is accompanied by Marguerite, his girlfriend whom he met at Kelsey's wedding on Cape Cod, and the ashes of both his parents, each urn riding in a separate wheel well in the trunk. His mother's passing has in no way diminished her presence in her son's life; Griffin is now literally haunted by his mother's voice interjecting, criticizing, and otherwise participating in his life. He hears her voice and responds to it—or turns up the radio to try to drown her out. These auditory hallucinations, which are rendered in italics, appear to take place, for the most part, in Griffin's head. But they contribute significantly to how he perceives and responds to others.

The second half of the novel, like the first, tells Griffin's story largely in flashback, with two large narrative sections anchoring the whole. The first, what Griffin comes to think of as the "Morphine Narrative," is the story his mother tells over the course of her last few days before her death, through her fog of powerful pain medication. She slowly reveals to Griffin a shocking and, in some ways, implausible tale of how she and his father remained lovers even after they divorced, and how their illicit relationship was much more exciting and enjoyable than their marriage had been. Griffin struggles to determine if she is telling the truth—if her story "tracks"—and although he wants to believe her tale, in the end he remains unsure. Certain details ring true, and others seem far-fetched, but most important, he comes to realize why she chose to reveal these secrets to him at all. She wants him to know that "*You never knew us. You thought you did, but how wrong you were. Our lives were a glorious secret, even from you*" (200). Even though he cannot be certain that the Morphine Narrative is true, Griffin does learn to appreciate that his understanding of his parents is incomplete and that certain aspects of their relationship were unavailable to him because of his immutable position as an outsider.

The second important flashback in part 2 involves Griffin's memories of his parents searching each year for the perfect Christmas tree. This reminiscence is prompted by Marguerite's request that Griffin tell her all about his parents so that she can understand them well enough to help him choose an appropriate site to scatter their ashes. Griffin starts by relaying mundane information about them—favorite colors, favorite foods, favorite times of day. But as he warms to the task, he begins telling her a long story about how his parents could never agree on the right Christmas tree, and how each year they would spend weeks dragging him to lot after lot, inspecting and rejecting tree after tree. After finally selecting one that was invariably too big for their house and struggling to fit it into the living room, they would trim it with borrowed decorations, and the young Griffin would crawl underneath it to look up into its glittering branches. By the end of this reminiscence, Griffin is surprised to find himself in tears; his long-overdue journey toward reconciling with his parents, even after their deaths, has clearly begun.

The wedding scene in part 2, the cornerstone of this half of the novel, begins with Griffin's and Joy's awkward reunion, followed by a rehearsal dinner that culminates in emergency room visits for most of the principals in the wedding party. Joy's father, Harve, now wheelchair-bound, manages to tip himself off the inn's wheelchair ramp into a ten-foot yew hedge; in the ensuing confusion Jared, who thinks that Griffin is somehow responsible for his father's predicament, punches Griffin in the eye and knocks him unconscious. The wheelchair ramp then collapses under the weight of so many onlookers, dumping many of them into the hedge and injuring several of them. Joy escapes with a broken finger and a gash on her side; Griffin has a concussion and an eye swelled nearly shut; Laura suffers an allergic reaction to the yew that makes her arms swell monstrously; and others emerge with bumps, bruises, and lacerations of all sorts. The comic absurdity of the scene is followed by continued chaos at the hospital, but there in the emergency room Griffin and Joy do find a few quiet moments together. For an instant their reconciliation seems imminent, but the encounter passes without a moment of grace, and Griffin returns to his inn, and to Marguerite.

Despite the rehearsal dinner's slapstick ending and the guests' lingering injuries, Laura's wedding goes off smoothly. Afterward, Griffin actually manages to scatter his parents' ashes (with Marguerite's help and support), and he begins thinking about their trip "home" to Los Angeles. But Marguerite knows better; she kindly releases him back to his old life, with the parting suggestion that he write a movie "with a girl like me in it" (256) and consider casting Susan Sarandon in the role. Once extricated from his affirming but ultimately purposeless liaison with Marguerite, Griffin considers reconciling with Joy. He reluctantly acknowledges to himself, "She'd been right all along that his parents, not hers, had intruded on their marriage with such disastrous consequences" (257). This jarring admission prompts him to swallow his pride, telephone Joy, and confess to her that he finally understands that he did love his parents despite their maddening ways. He also screws up the nerve to ask if he has entirely destroyed their marriage and is overwhelmed with relief to learn that "only the part that could be killed" (260) was dead but that the rest was still salvageable. Their reunion ensured, Griffin can finally tell his deceased mother, who has never stopped haunting him, "*I think maybe I'm going to be okay, Mom. . . . I guess what I'm saying is that it's okay for you to be dead now*" (260). Thus, it seems, fate pulls the "congenitally unhappy" Griffin back from the brink of despair and divorce, rescues him from his late mother's incessant haunting, and offers him one more chance at happiness.

That Old Cape Magic functions in many ways as a thorough revisiting of *Straight Man*, but with the satire considerably dialed down. The parallels between the two novels are numerous. Jack Griffin and Hank Devereaux are both middle-aged creative-writing professors, the only sons of high-achieving academic parents who were intensely dissatisfied with their professional lives and, as a result, faced their world with cynicism and scorn. The expectations of both the elder Griffins and the elder Devereaux were impossible to live up to (which they made clear to their sons), even as they proved themselves completely unworthy of emulation. Nevertheless both Griffin and Hank end up as college professors, even as they try desperately to distance themselves from their parents. Although Hank revels in his lack of academic productivity (one published novel, no Ph.D., no aspirations otherwise), he cringes at his physical likeness to his father, while Griffin chafes when he thinks about how much he has come to resemble his father in both appearance and behavior. Both the senior and junior Griffins physically freeze up when they cannot make a decision ("his father's classic pose" [5]), and they both absentmindedly misplace student papers (William Griffin was "famous for losing student work" [42]). Also like his father, Jack Griffin never feels successful or comfortable in his professorial career; both of them seem to be looking for the next opportunity to leave the current situation behind. Griffin and Hank both have trouble dealing with the long shadow their parents cast over their lives and in their middle age still struggle to understand their complicated feelings toward them that began in childhood and remain largely unresolved.

Griffin and Hank also share a deep self-absorption, to the extent that they have trouble connecting even to those closest to them. Nevertheless each of them manages to marry generous, talented, patient women who do their best to put up with their husbands' eccentricities, and both Joy Griffin and Lily Devereaux are sorely tested in the process. Both men raise daughters who, even into adulthood, remain terrified that their parents will divorce (Karen Devereaux's worst fears remain unrealized, while Laura Griffin suffers through her parents' yearlong separation). Both Griffin and Hank experience what might commonly be termed "midlife crises," though the actual nature of each character's crisis takes a rather different form. In addition both men prove themselves to be thoroughly unreliable interpreters of their own experiences. However, while Hank's first-person narration in *Straight Man* presents itself as unreliable almost from the start, the close third-person narration in *That Old Cape Magic* allows readers to be distracted, at least temporarily, from Griffin's lack of self-awareness.

The first chapter of *That Old Cape Magic,* "A Finer Place," seems to suggest, initially, that Cape Cod is that finer place. The chapter, however, includes revealing details of Griffin's parents' annual Cape Cod real-estate wrangle that indicate the finer place may exist more in the imagination than in the classifieds. Upon arriving each summer at their rented cottage, "a single day was usually all it took for each of them to plow through the hundreds of listings in the fat real-estate guide and place each into one of two categories—Can't Afford It or Wouldn't Have It As a Gift" (10). Despite their longtime aspiration to buy a vacation/retirement home on the Cape, all their dreams seem to exist in some vague, uncertain, future place that cannot even be identified, let alone purchased. Although Griffin persists in thinking about his parents' experiences on the Cape as the locus of their happiness, "as if happiness were a place" (16), it quickly becomes clear that they were perpetually mired in their present unhappiness. Unfortunately, Griffin inherits this trait and internalizes this binary attitude of "Can't Afford It" versus "Wouldn't Have It As a Gift"; as an adult he unconsciously applies it to aspects of his life that transcend mere real estate. His own lack of awareness of his negativity and dissatisfaction with his life blinds readers, at least initially, to the fact that, as the reviewer Brooke Allen noted, Griffin "is not the nicest guy in the world, and he has been unconscionably hard on Joy."[4]

Griffin's "unconscionably hard" treatment of his wife is an element of the narrative that emerges gradually, since Griffin himself remains mostly unaware of his transgressions. He believes that he loves his wife, yet repeated examples of his selfishness and pettiness, including his inability to back down from an argument and his extreme reluctance to apologize to her, make it apparent that he may not be the good husband he imagines himself to be. Joy tends to interpret his behavior generously, suggesting that "he had too little faith—in the world, in her, in himself, in their good lives—and sometimes got important things wrong as a result" (119). What Griffin does not realize until late in the novel is that his lack of faith in "their good lives" results from his assimilation of his parents' pretensions. His mother never thought that Joy was good enough for Griffin and felt that he was wasting his intellect and his talents. Her entire worldview crystallizes in the spiteful assertion she makes about her granddaughter, Laura: "Only very stupid people are happy" (195). But this attitude has long been coalescing in Griffin's psyche, and it has inevitably influenced his feelings toward Joy, who has tried her best to live a happy life and to make him happy too. He does not want to believe that he interprets Joy's optimism, her adaptability, her "ability to still want what she wanted so long ago" as shortcomings, and yet he cannot help feeling that perhaps "her contentment was the true cause of his funk" (83). This tentative acknowledgment that other people's happiness makes Griffin unhappy suggests the depths of the damage his parents have inflicted, but still he cannot understand just how he has become the person he is.

Overall, Griffin's most significant blind spot is that he cannot recognize the extent to which he has actually become like his parents. He never equates his parents' annual summer exodus from Indiana to Cape Cod with his own "long-established habit to flee the campus as soon as [he] taught his last class" (3), seeking the pleasures of New York City as eagerly as his parents anticipated crossing the bridge onto the Cape. He does not understand that he is channeling his parents' disdain for Joy's family when he mocks them, referring to Harve as "Jarve," for example, since all the rest of them have names that start with J, or calling Joy's sister "Princess Grace of Morocco" after she makes a mistake in a game of charades. In addition Griffin's secret efforts to resurrect his old screen-writing career, through phone calls he makes

to his agent and to his partner when Joy is out of earshot, echo the duplici-
tous nature of his parents' unhappy marriage. Griffin is far from the only
Russo character in danger of repeating the mistakes of his parents; Ned Hall
in *The Risk Pool* knows all too well how easy it is to fall into the destructive
patterns of his father, and Lucy Lynch in *Bridge of Sighs* learns that emulat-
ing Big Lou too closely can endanger his own marriage to Sarah. But Griffin's
profound lack of awareness regarding his parents' pervasive influence on
his behavior and attitudes sets him apart from other Russo characters. He
believes his parents to be poisonous influences and feels certain that he has
managed to sequester them and their snobbish cynicism away from himself
and his family, to a place where they cannot do any harm. Yet he does not
realize that he himself has become a conduit for their snobbery and cynicism,
and thus he has not actually shielded his family from anything. In fact he
unwittingly enacts many of the very behaviors he condemns in his parents,
not recognizing that he has effectively absorbed his parents' perpetual dissatisfaction with life. Joy accuses Griffin of being "congenitally unhappy,"
but his lack of self-awareness prevents him from understanding why.

Griffin's epiphany comes late in the novel, when it is nearly too late to
save his marriage, and takes the form of an admission that Joy finds glar-
ingly, painfully obvious. The two of them have begun their separate drives
home from Laura's wedding when Griffin finds himself involved in a minor
car accident reminiscent of the dozens of such fender benders his father had
caused. In a fumbled attempt to call the police, Griffin accidentally calls
Joy's cell phone, and when she answers, he recognizes that "this might just
be the moment of grace he'd been waiting for" (259). He stumbles around
awkwardly before finally bringing himself to ask her the question about
his parents that has been unconsciously gnawing at him: "'Since yesterday,
maybe for awhile [*sic*] before that, I've been wondering . . .' He stopped here,
unsure how to continue, though what he'd been wondering couldn't have
been simpler. 'I've been wondering if maybe I loved them. It's crazy, I know,
but . . . do you think that's possible?'" Joy answers immediately, "Of course
you did. What do you think I've been trying to tell you?" (259), and Griffin's
admission of love for his parents, however hard it was to reach, creates for
the estranged couple a path that can lead them back together. Griffin realizes
that he can love his parents even if he hates their attitudes or disagrees with
their conclusions, and it is this unacknowledged love, finally acknowledged,
that permits Griffin to escape his parents' powerful grip. The haunting voice
of his mother grows silent, and a circling seagull, in the first chapter a symbol
of his mother's omnipresent nastiness, in the final moments of the book flies
harmlessly away.

One particularly insightful reviewer identified the crux of *That Old Cape Magic* through a series of questions about the legacy of "caustic parents," who, she recognized, "may be the hardest to leave behind." The reviewer asked, "Can we see them for what they are and yet admit that we love them? Can we learn to laugh at and deal with our resemblance to them? And, most crucial of all, can we live lives of love and contentment even while we recognize the imperfections and uncertainties that haunt all of our relationships and endeavors?"[5] Griffin is unable to imagine these questions, let alone answer them, until his marriage and his whole future are seriously threatened. While his first deliberate response to such questions would likely have been in all cases negative, his development throughout the novel indicates that by the conclusion, he realizes that all the answers are actually "yes." Only through Griffin's growing self-awareness can he recognize his love for his parents and, at the same time, prevent their legacy of bitterness from tainting his future.

In general, reviews of *That Old Cape Magic* were positive, and its 2009 summertime release (coupled with the beach-themed cover art) positioned it well for inclusion on lists of summer "beach reading." Thus many early reviews of the novel seemed to consider the question of its suitability for such lists, with the consensus emerging that its relatively short length and funny subplots, especially those involving Griffin's parents, made it a fine choice. Most reviewers appreciated how much the novel's comic sequences effectively leaven an otherwise somber story line; one described Russo's depiction of Mary and William Griffin this way: "Insufferably snobbish, unkind, competitive and self-destructive, they are also vivid and hilarious. Russo . . . names Charles Dickens as one of his primary literary influences, and the elder Griffins take their place with the likes of Mr. Dorrit and Miss Havisham."[6] Others acknowledged that the tone of *That Old Cape Magic* differs markedly from Russo's more comic works. The *Library Journal* review, for example, called the novel a loving exploration of "the deceptive nature of memory as each exquisitely drawn character attempts to deconstruct the family myths that inform their relationships."[7] Most reviewers, in fact, emphasized the centrality of relationships in *That Old Cape Magic;* one such review claimed, "The tightness of the novel's structure belies the profound contemplation of family—childhood, parenthood, friendship, marriage—packed into this crucial year of Griffin's life, a year when he undergoes what nowadays we still call a 'midlife' crisis, even when it happens to someone who is 57."[8]

Readers of *That Old Cape Magic* can also identify thematic connections to Russo's previous novels. The notion of luck, for example, which figures so prominently in *Nobody's Fool* and *Straight Man,* emerges here in Tommy's repeated assertion that Griffin is "Mr. Lucky" but without the good sense to appreciate it. Failed or failing marriages, which appear in virtually all of Russo's fiction, surface in the form of Griffin and Joy's rocky relationship as well as in William and Mary Griffin's disastrous marriage and, surprisingly, Jill's posthumously revealed extramarital affair. But most important, in *That Old Cape Magic*, Russo returns once again to his most ubiquitous theme: the difficulty of establishing and nurturing healthy relationships between parents and children. Not a single novel in Russo's body of work neglects this subject; everywhere in Russo's literary landscape we see parents and children disappointing each other, hurting each other, breaking each other's hearts. Some fractures never heal; Randall Younger, for example, never fully connects with his father, Dallas, in *Mohawk*, and Sully never forgives his abusive father, Big Jim, in *Nobody's Fool*. But most difficult relationships evolve into some kind of truce, even if that truce takes decades to reach. Ned Hall reconciles with his father before Sam succumbs to cancer in *The Risk Pool*, and Miles and Max Roby seem to understand each other better by the end of *Empire Falls*, as do Lucy and his mother, Tessa, at the conclusion of *Bridge of Sighs*. But Griffin's healing process is unique in that it does not truly begin until after his parents' deaths. While they were living, he was intent on disavowing their influence altogether. He acknowledges his primary problem in that "you could put a couple thousand miles between yourself and your parents, and make it clear to them that in doing so you meant to reject their values, but how did you distance yourself from your own inheritance?" (70). The obvious answer, which takes Griffin a lifetime to learn, is that one simply cannot escape one's inheritance. Children inevitably carry their parents' influences forward into their adult lives; the question is not how to prevent this but how to cope with it in a healthy, deliberate way. For Griffin, this process took years of denial, followed by a serious examination of his feelings about both his late parents and his wife. His ultimate triumph, Russo suggests, means that it is never too late to make peace with the past.

CHAPTER 9

Other Works

As of 2014 Richard Russo's output is dominated by his seven novels, but to that total must be added two collections of short fiction, *The Whore's Child and Other Stories* (2002) and *Interventions: A Novella & Three Stories* (2012); a memoir, *Elsewhere* (2012); a novella, *Nate in Venice* (2013); and a large assortment of short nonfiction pieces that he has contributed to various collections or, in a few cases, published separately. In addition he has composed many articles and reviews as well as introductions, forewords, and afterwards for volumes written or edited by other writers. (Please see the bibliography for more details.)

The Whore's Child and Other Stories (2002)

"Reading a collection of Richard Russo stories," one critic remarked, "is like watching a home-run hitter try to lay down a squeeze bunt."[1] In other words, the expansive worlds that Russo develops in his long novels, full of large casts of characters, involved personal histories, and multiple subplots, are sacrificed in his short fiction for mere glimpses of these worlds and their inhabitants. Further, the comic touch that defines most of Russo's novels is conspicuously absent in *The Whore's Child and Other Stories;* witty moments do surface from time to time—a clever retort, a humorous juxtaposition— but the tales in this collection are much darker and more serious than Russo's novels. With a few exceptions, the stories focus on middle-aged (or older) characters who come to feel deeply ambivalent about their marriages or the slow but persistent decline of their lives' trajectories, including a loss of passion for the people who once meant everything to them.

Of the seven stories included in *The Whore's Child and Other Stories,* Russo acknowledged in a 2011 interview that one "is actually a novella, so it's not even a short story. Three of the stories in that collection are actually outtakes from my novels, parts that I couldn't fit in. I have really only just three or four examples of stories that started out as stories and ended up stories."[2] "The Mysteries of Linwood Hart" was taken in part from a draft of *Empire Falls*, where it was intended to help explain Miles Roby's trip to Martha's Vineyard as a child but was ultimately seen as too much of a digression from the heart of the novel. "The Farther You Go" actually inspired *Straight Man;* "The Whore's Child" was originally included in a draft of *Straight Man,* but in the end Russo and his editor agreed to remove Sister Ursula's story from the novel. But then, Russo explained, he was so fond of the character that "[I] created a story around her because I couldn't bear not to have her doing something."[3] Russo admitted that the short-story form is difficult for him; he typically finds himself chafing under a twenty-five- or thirty-page limit and that sometimes pieces that start out as short stories actually end up as novels, which is what happened with *That Old Cape Magic*. Although his first published pieces were short stories and he has admitted to being a tremendous fan of the genre, it took him many years to release a collection of short fiction because he simply lacked sufficient stories that he thought merited publication in such a format.

The Whore's Child and Other Stories was released in the wake of the 2002 Pulitzer Prize for fiction being awarded to *Empire Falls*, and as a result the collection garnered considerable attention. It was reviewed widely and for the most part favorably. Reviewers familiar with Russo's novels often commented on the thematic connections between his longer works and the stories in this collection; one reviewer observed that the concerns of the professional types included in *The Whore's Child and Other Stories*, largely artists, writers, and professors, "are not so different from the blue-collar folk of *Nobody's Fool* or *Empire Falls*: the advance of age; the fleeting joys and inevitable complications of love, marriage, and children."[4] The novelist Francine Prose commented, "[Russo] has the quiet authority of someone with a valuable story to tell, a story about ordinary people in the extraordinary circumstances we recognize as normal existence. . . . It's an admirable achievement to make these well-crafted and deftly plotted tales seem as unlikely and as plausible as your life."[5] Peter Heinegg concluded his laudatory review this way: "There are no stylistic pyrotechnics, à la John Updike, no convoluted allegories of ego, à la Philip Roth, just quirky, meandering, anticlimactic narratives with pitch-perfect dialogue about a bunch of ordinary male, female, and pre-adolescent losers, who happen to inhabit certain neighborhoods in the Northeast, but who end up looking alarmingly (grin and bear it) like the rest of us."[6]

In "The Whore's Child," the first and title story, the unnamed first-person narrator is a creative-writing teacher at an unidentified university who has recently published a successful book, and as a result, his creative writing class is oversubscribed. Nevertheless he allows an elderly nun, Sister Ursula of St. Francis's Church, to attend his class, not because she followed any element of university procedure to enroll properly (she did not), nor because she is qualified to take the class (she is not), but rather because she gives off the strong impression that she has no intention of leaving. Her body language, the narrator notes, indicates that "once settled, she was not used to moving. And since she was clearly settled, I let her stay" (5).

The bulk of the story concerns the back-and-forth exchanges between Sister Ursula and her teacher, with the autobiographical story the nun sets out to write serving as the conduit between them. Her story is retold through the filter of the narrator, who does not quote from her work, except for her rather exceptional opening lines, but rather paraphrases the general plot direction of the tale. Sister Ursula is the "whore's child" of the title; as the young daughter of a prostitute, she was brought to a Belgian convent school by her father, a man she saw only once more in her life, during a Christmas holiday during her first year at the convent. Her memoir details the cruelties she suffered at the hands of the nuns and her classmates as a "charity case" in the convent and traces her life as one full of hatred and disappointment. Her prostitute mother dies in a charity hospital; her father is never heard from again. At sixteen she takes her vows to become a nun; some years later, when her convent partially burns down, she relocates to the United States. Although she returns once to Belgium to seek her father, she never finds him.

The entire story plays with the idea of storytelling and how to tell a good story. After each installment of Sister Ursula's tale is submitted to the class, the narrator relays the responses of the other students in the workshop. Their critiques follow the paths set out for them in a creative-writing class— notions of plot, characterization, expectations of the readers, and a sense of betrayal when those expectations are violated. Thus the complexity of the craft of storytelling is juxtaposed with the single-mindedness of the story-teller, Sister Ursula, who has no use for such academic insights but rather aches to unburden herself of this tale while she still can.

The twist of the story comes near the end, during Sister Ursula's final workshop session. In the memoir the "whore's child" reveals a lifelong yearning for her father and an almost worshipful feeling toward him. She blames her mother for ruining her father's life and for her own subsequent separation from him, and yet she seems to have no insight into her father's character or circumstances. Another student in the workshop, "her eyes brimming with tears," offers the observation that changes Sister Ursula's life and opens her eyes to the implications of her own story that she has been unable to see on her own. The student asks Sister Ursula, "He was the mother's pimp, right? Is there another explanation?" (21). Clearly the details of the story offer no other plausible explanation, although Sister Ursula has never once considered this possibility.

"Monhegan Light," first published in *Esquire* magazine, takes the reader to an artists' colony on remote Monhegan Island, off the coast of Maine. "Monhegan Light" tells the story of Martin, a Hollywood gaffer-turned-director-of-photography, and his journey to Monhegan Island. When Martin receives a nude painting of his late wife, Laura, he realizes that she and the painter, Robert Trevor, must have been lovers. Armed with Trevor's address at the artists' colony on Monhegan, Martin sets out, with his beautiful, much-younger girlfriend in tow, to face the man who painted this portrait and who, he infers, meant so much to his late wife. Martin's worst suspicions are confirmed when Trevor admits that Laura was his muse and that the two of them were lovers for twenty summers. Martin is stunned, however, when Trevor claims that the person Laura actually longed for all her life was not him but was, in fact, Martin.

"Monhegan Light" plays on the word "light" in several respects. The 1824 Monhegan Island Light, an iconic lighthouse, often appears in tourism brochures and Web sites for the island, but the story barely mentions the lighthouse. The light on Monhegan is mentioned in Martin's and Robert Trevor's first encounter, when Trevor is trying to paint in the fading afternoon light and searches for the Hollywood term "magic hour" to describe the last hour of daylight. Symbolically, though, the Monhegan light represents Martin's epiphany as he comes to terms not only with his late wife's long-term affair but also with his newly engendered feelings of love for Laura as he begins to see her from Trevor's perspective.

"The Farther You Go," originally published in *Shenandoah,* tells the story of Hank, a fifty-two-year-old father recovering from prostate surgery, who is assigned the awkward task of running his son-in-law, Russell, out of town. Russell and his wife Julie have a turbulent marriage, and after Russell strikes Julie, Hank is called upon by his daughter to set things right. Hank's fondness for Russell notwithstanding, he does as he is asked and puts Russell on the road to Pittsburgh. The story, told from Hank's point of view and consisting mostly of interior narration, reveals more about Hank's own marriage and his feelings as a father than it does about anything else, including Russell's and Julie's current situation and possible future. Hank believes that his wife, Faye, does not know him well, and he admits that he has never made a point to be honest with her. Yet in the end, Faye comes unbidden to the airport to pick up Hank after she surmises that he would need a ride home. When she asks him, "Don't you think I know you after thirty years?" the answer she presumes is "yes"; when he answers "not intimately," she assumes that he is making a joke about his recent surgery for prostate cancer and jokes back, "Hurry up and mend then" (72). But the implication for the reader is that Hank really does not believe that Faye knows him, though her actions at the end suggest that she at least knows him well enough to predict his behaviors, if not his thoughts.

"The Farther You Go" became the seed for *Straight Man* (1997), a novel about English professor Hank Devereaux, and several of the characters in the story reappear in the novel in fuller form. In fact this very scene is repeated in *Straight Man*, with slight revisions to better fit the context of the novel. Russo explained in a 2002 interview that after he wrote "The Farther You Go," "[I] liked the character [of Hank] so much and I couldn't let him go. I then went back and wrote *Straight Man* around that character."[7]

The story "Joy Ride," originally published in *Meridian*, is told from the perspective of twelve-year-old John Dern, whose mother one day unexpectedly shuffles him out of bed and into a cross-country road trip, leaving behind a one-word note, "Goodbye," to her husband. The ensuing "joy ride" takes mother and son to truck stops and cheap motels on an intended journey to southern California, where, as John notes, his mother intends "to lose my father and lose him good" (74). However, bad luck, including a vandalized car and an attempted rape, causes John's mother to question her resolve, and by the time they get to the Southwest, she points the car not toward the California coast but rather toward her parents' trailer in Phoenix, Arizona. From there the story shifts forward more than twenty years, as John recounts their flight back to Maine, his father's warm welcome, and his mother's insistence, over the years, on remembering their trip not as an escape from her husband but rather as a planned vacation meant to separate young John from his undesirable group of hoodlum friends. The final moments of the story suggest, however, that his mother's denial of the real intent of the "joy ride" is deliberate and that she too knows the truth.

"Buoyancy," first published in John McNally's edited collection *High Infidelity* (1997), revisits the common Russo theme of a fractured marriage, this time from the point of view of the husband, who feels remote and disconnected from his wife of many years. In the story Professor Paul Snow and his wife, June, travel to Martha's Vineyard, a place they had visited together thirty years before, just after they were married. This time, though, the trip is colored by the newly retired Professor Snow's hypersensitivity to his wife's state of mind, a sensitivity he has felt since she suffered a nervous break-down a few years before. The couple decides to spend a day on the clothing-optional beach at Gay Head, and in an unanticipated show of daring, June removes her bathing suit to sunbathe. Paul follows suit, and when he awakens from his nap to find himself badly sunburned and June missing, he begins a disoriented, ill-fated search for her. Paul, in a state of near collapse, is rescued by a young couple who lead him along the beach in search of June. When they find her, the dazed and ill Paul says "something so cruel that it was easy. 'Cover yourself, June,' he'd instructed her. 'For God's sake'" (142).

The story reveals, through Paul's memory, three decades of troubled marriage, brought to the fore by his recollection of June's revelation of how unhappy she has been in their marriage and how she took revenge for his infidelity by taking a lover of her own. Their uneasy peace as they travel to Martha's Vineyard is easily shattered, and at the end of the story readers understand how deeply Paul and June despair at their inability to connect honestly with one another.

Another island story, "Poison," originally published in *Kiosk,* depicts the reunion of two writers who hail from the same small industrial town. The narrator has enjoyed some financial success as a Hollywood screenwriter and, as a result, can now afford to own an island cottage, presumably, though not explicitly stated, on Martha's Vineyard. His friend Gene Ruggieri has not been as successful, in part, it seems, because of his obsession with his mill-town past and his father's role, as a foreman, of contributing to the poisoning of mill workers, including the narrator's father. The story explores how two people from the same background can come to see their world, and their past, in dramatically different ways. It also hits on one of Russo's favorite themes, expressed by Gene's sarcastic young wife, who declares of her husband's ratty sweater, "It means he's a proletarian writer laboring in the sweatshop of tough, honest prose. It means he comes from an ugly mill town and that's who he is and always will be" (153).

A scene in "Poison" repeats a nearly identical moment in *Mohawk.* In "Poison" the narrator recalls a conversation with his father about the mill's role in his cancer. His father says, "It's true they poisoned me. But where would a man like me have been without that mill?" (165). In *Mohawk,* Rory Gaffney directs a similar question to Mr. Anadio, who has contracted cancer after working in the tanneries. Gaffney says, "If I *was* sick, I'd thank the shops anyway. Where would men like us have been without work?" (200). In both cases blue-collar workers appear to acknowledge that mill work comes with inevitable and sometimes fatal tradeoffs, and that even knowing the dangers of working in such industries would likely not have prevented "men like us" from taking the jobs and providing for their families. Gene Ruggieri, however, who does not have cancer, feels complicit in the criminal neglect of the mill for its workers' health and safety, and he suffers tremendous guilt. His vision extends only to the past, and his dream, which he invites the reluctant narrator to share, is to find a way to shutter for good the mill that poisoned so many workers.

"The Mysteries of Linwood Hart," the final and by far the longest story in the collection, originated as part of *Empire Falls*. The story follows ten-year-old Linwood "Lin" Hart, a boy who, according to his teachers, "possesses an active interior life" (171), as he watches the dissolution and then the sudden restoration of his parents' marriage. An "active interior life" is a significant understatement, as much of the story exposes the complicated workings of Lin's imagination and the poignant questions he poses to himself as he tries to understand his life and his role within his family. As in other Russo stories that adopt a child's perspective, "The Mysteries of Linwood Hart" explores the mysteries of adult behavior as seen through the eyes of a child, and Lin slowly begins to make sense of his parents' separation, his father's fractious relationship with his family, and his mother's relationship with Lin's new baseball coach. When the story opens, Lin considers himself special in the way and to the degree that most children do. When his mother sarcastically asks him, "What do you think you are? Special?," Lin thinks to himself that even though the answer was supposed to be "no," he could not help but think that "it might be 'Yes'" (172). By the end of the story, though, he has reached a new level of understanding about life that makes him feel as if he has entered a brand new world. The story closes, "It was into this entirely different world that Linwood Hart now fell asleep, sadly grateful that he was not and never had been, nor ever would be, its center" (225). This ending may seem a bit overwritten; one reviewer suggested that "you can't help thinking the story would be better with some of this [heavy-handed narrative] left out." But this same reviewer also noted that the story succeeds overall because of Russo's "sure grasp of paradox: that to imagine the limitations of your imagination is to begin to comprehend the world beyond childhood."[8]

A Healing Touch: True Stories of Life, Death, and Hospice (2008)

In 2008 Russo released his first and, to date, only edited collection of essays, *A Healing Touch: True Stories of Life, Death, and Hospice;* he wrote a brief introduction to the collection and contributed one of its six essays. The volume was conceived to raise funds for the Hospice Volunteers of the Waterville Area (HVWA), an organization serving Waterville, Maine, and twenty-seven other area communities. Each of the six contributing writers is a Maine author, and their stories describe the impact that hospice care has had on their friends or family members. Russo's contribution, a first-person narrative titled "You Know Who You Are," details the story of his friend Lee Duff and the challenges Lee faced when his beloved wife Ann fell victim to Alzheimer's disease. The story blends flashbacks of Lee's and Ann's childhoods, early courtship, and married life with details of Lee's more recent struggles to cope with Ann's illness and, finally, his life after her death as well as his role as a volunteer and leader in the HVWA.

"You Know Who You Are" is one of few nonfiction essays that Russo has published. Although the goal of the collection is to convey the real-life stories of families whose lives intersect in some ways with the mission of HVWA, Russo employs a number of strategies common to his fiction in order to tell the poignant story of the Duffs and their struggles. For example, he reveals the central conflict in this story slowly; readers do not learn that Ann Duff is afflicted by Alzheimer's until about a dozen pages into the piece, and at first it seems the story is going to be about Lee's impending health issues. Russo conveys the heartbreaking nature of the Duffs' situation without sentimentality or maudlin emotion; rather he balances his storytelling craft with sincerity and respect for his friends and their seemingly impossible and tragic situation.

Interventions: A Novella & Three Stories (2012)

Interventions is a collection of four short pieces, each published as a separate book and inserted in a single slipcase. Russo and his collaborator, his younger daughter, the artist Kate Russo, call it "a tribute to the printed word." Each of the four works, "Intervention," "The Whore's Child," "High and Dry," and "Horseman," is accompanied by an original color print by his daughter. The longest of the pieces, "Intervention," is the only previously unpublished work in the collection.

The appearance of Interventions coincided with Russo's very public pushback against Amazon.com, which he believes is a "predatory" force that "puts young writers in peril."[9] Russo maintains that online book browsing by key words tends to yield results that privilege older, more established, usually best-selling authors. Employees of independent booksellers, however, can steer readers toward newer books by lesser-known writers.[10] Russo also decries what the online retail industry calls "showrooming," which encourages shoppers to browse brick-and-mortar stores but then buy online for lower prices and often no sales tax. Mobile phone apps make it easy to scan bar codes and find lower prices at sites such as Amazon.com, and Russo believes that this practice is decimating independent booksellers. His elder daughter, Emily, is an independent bookseller at Greenlight Bookstore in Brooklyn, New York (as of 2014), and so this argument hits close to home for him and his family.

All four of the stories collected in *Interventions* contain, as Russo has noted, a kind of intervention, "some element in which an outside force profoundly intervenes in someone's life."[11] To amplify this theme in the three previously published stories and provide some cohesion among them, Russo composed "Intervention," which tells the story of Ray, a realtor in coastal Maine battling a stagnant real-estate market, unresolved issues with his long-dead relatives, and a recent cancer diagnosis. In certain ways Ray appears to be a familiar Russo character—a middle-aged man from a blue-collar background struggling to accept the realities that come with aging and to make sense of his unsettled relationship with his late father. Unlike many other Russo protagonists, though, Ray has a solid, loving marriage with Paula, and their quiet but abiding love anchors the story.

The story is full of literal interventions—actions taken (without permission) by some characters to help others. Ray intervenes in his friend Nicki's life by rearranging her many belongings to help her house sell, at a time when she feels so paralyzed by victimization and depression that she cannot seem to take any actions to help herself. Ray's and Paula's friend Vinnie intervenes to provide a connection to a prominent oncologist in Boston, and Paula then makes an appointment with the doctor for Ray without his permission. In flashbacks to Ray's childhood, readers learn that his Uncle Jack tried repeatedly to intervene in Ray's father's mundane factory life by offering him a share in a variety of "get-rich-quick" schemes. These offers were firmly rejected each time, but Uncle Jack kept returning with new opportunities until finally Ray's father beat him up, thus permanently severing their relationship and, perhaps, a developing romantic relationship between Jack and Rita, Ray's mother. In all these cases the characters reach moments in their lives when they can no longer rely only on themselves; they require interventions by others if they are to move forward.

"Intervention" illustrates how individuals cannot always come to grips with their own obsessions and so other people who have more realistic and objective perspectives on the situations must be ready and willing to intercede. Nicki's problem of the cluttered house is far from unsolvable; in fact Ray and Vinnie manage to solve it in about two hours by hauling out her many boxes to the garage and immediately making her house more appealing to potential buyers. But it is unsolvable to Nicki. Likewise, Ray cannot deal rationally with his cancer diagnosis; he saw his father receive his own diagnosis passively, without complaint, and now he cannot fathom a different reaction, one that would involve actively engaging with the situation. Paula's ability to understand Ray's need, to see things about him that he refuses to see himself, and her willingness to intervene when he needs her demonstrate the strength of their relationship and suggest a real reason for him to have hope for his future. Indeed in the closing moments of the story, Ray acknowledges feeling "a cautious hope" (67) that everything would work out in the end and that this would not be his last Maine winter.

"The Whore's Child," the title piece in Russo's 2002 short-story collection and reprinted in *Interventions*, provides at least two opportunities for readers to appreciate the power of an interloper who can provide much-needed insight into a situation. Sister Ursula arrives in the narrator's creative-writing class certain that she understands the autobiographical story she wants to tell and needs only the opportunity to tell it. But ultimately she cannot see or understand things about her own life story without the intervention of an outside reader, in this case a fellow student trying to offer constructive feedback during a collaborative workshop session. Sister Ursula has wrestled for years with her deep hatred of her mother, a prostitute who died of syphilis, and her abiding love for her "tall, handsome father who had promised to rescue her from this place as soon as he could find work" (12) but who in the end abandons her at the convent school and disappears from her life without a trace. What Sister Ursula could not see for herself is the fact that her father was, in all likelihood, her mother's pimp. "Is there another explanation?" (29), asks the young woman in the class, and indeed there is not. Although painful to face, this intervention allows the elderly nun to see her past in focus for the first time.

But Sister Ursula's experience with her insightful classmate is not the only intervention in the story; indeed the narrator experiences Sister Ursula's presence in his class as a kind of intervention. In working out how to deal with this most nontraditional of students, he finds himself able to see his own failed marriage through clearer eyes. He longs to confide in Sister Ursula, to admit to her, "I am not a good man. . . . I have not only failed, but also betrayed those I love" (32). The narrator never gets over feeling at least slightly uncomfortable around the nun, and perhaps her uneasy presence in his life helps him face his own uncomfortable truths about his meaningless adulterous affair and its terrible cost to himself, his wife, and their daughter.

"High and Dry," Russo's first published piece of extended autobiographical writing, originally appeared in *Granta* in 2010 and was later included in slightly altered form in *Elsewhere* (2012). In it he offers a brief history of his hometown of Gloversville, New York, which in its heyday produced 90 percent of the dress gloves manufactured in the United States. When Russo was a boy in the 1950s, throngs of shoppers jammed the downtown sidewalks, and the town bustled with energy and prosperity. But by the 1960s outsourcing glove production to cheap Asian manufacturers basically shuttered the factories and tanneries of Gloversville, and by the time he graduated from high school in 1967, Russo writes, "you could have strafed Main Street with automatic weapon fire without endangering a soul" (14). Throughout the essay Russo reckons with his feelings toward Gloversville as they have evolved over the course of his life, and he faces the guilt he feels for having escaped the circumscribed life of dead-end factory work or road construction to which he would have been heir had he remained in his hometown.

In "High and Dry," Russo describes celebrating his younger daughter's 2007 wedding in London, where he and other guests swap stories about working bad jobs. Russo shares a story about working a nonunion construction job while he was home from college one summer; although the job was awful and potentially dangerous, it was only temporary and he lived to tell a funny story about it. His cousin Greg's job in the beam house of a skin mill, however, easily eclipses Russo's in both nastiness and poignancy, for it includes not just the unpleasantness of the work but also how it dehumanizes the workers, compromising their standards of cleanliness and, finally, even decency. The survivor's guilt that Russo feels as he relates the horrific tales of work in the skin mills crystallizes when he remembers how "sometimes, late in August, working road construction with my father, I'd think about not going back to college and maybe just staying on to do that hard, honest work he and his friends did all year round" (36). In merely recalling that temptation to lead a workingman's life, Russo describes the guilt he feels, "like I've cheated destiny or, worse, swapped destinies with some other poor sod—to be where I am" (36).

"High and Dry" was originally written for inclusion in a special 2010 issue of *Granta* dedicated to the idea of "going home," but Russo resisted writing the piece until he was sure that he would be able do it without actually traveling back to Gloversville. His homecoming would be, he told his editor, "strictly metaphorical."[12] Nevertheless he worked diligently to get the details of his hometown correct—a problem he did not have when writing about fictional versions of Gloversville in his novels. Russo explained in a 2010 interview that while he was composing "High and Dry," "I realized I had a responsibility not to the kind of truth that I normally strive for, but to the literal truth of real people's lives. It made me careful, cautious; it made me absolutely want to get things as right as I could, because I was writing about people's lives, people who had real names and had experienced what I was writing about secondhand. I had to get it literally right, making sure that their names were spelled correctly, making sure that I understood that part of this was about the kind of lives, the really dangerous lives, that people lived working in the tanneries where I grew up."[13] The epiphany in "High and Dry" comes at the end of the essay, when Russo finally acknowledges to himself the depth and intensity of his connection to Gloversville, and that despite his long absence from the town, he understands it is "the only place I've ever called home and meant by that what people mean who never leave" (50).

"Horseman" first appeared in a 2006 *Atlantic* fiction issue and is the fourth and final piece included in *Interventions*. It focuses on Janet Moore, a tenured literature professor at an unidentified college, who has a disabled, perhaps autistic son; a saintly, underappreciated husband; and a ghost in the form of a graduate school professor from her past. Professor Marcus Bellamy, for whom her son is named, was a towering literary personality who figured only briefly in her academic life, but Janet never recovered from this particular "intervention." While Janet was a graduate student, Bellamy accused her of lacking true passion, of the inability to infuse her academic work with a true sense of herself, and claimed that she was somehow absent from the products of her own mind. He concluded his assessment of her scholarly potential with a damning, yet somehow prophetic pronouncement to Janet that "you'll succeed just fine . . . [y]ou'll just never be any good" (25). Indeed ten years later she has achieved certain trappings of professional and personal success—her tenured position, her tested-but-still-enduring marriage—but seems to believe that deep down Bellamy was right and she really is not "any good."

In the story's present, Janet feels overwhelmed by the demands of her job and her family; she must deal with an annoying case of plagiarism by an unrepentant student, and the approaching Thanksgiving holiday promises to be challenging for her disabled son. She is still haunted by Bellamy's prophecy, which manifests itself through the constant refrain in her head of Robert Louis Stevenson's "Windy Nights," a children's poem that her husband, Robbie, reads to their son, Marcus, every night. The poem once surfaced, during a long-ago drunken celebration, as Bellamy's pick for the greatest poem in the English language because, as he cryptically put it, "when I speak those words aloud, my father is alive again" (53). Janet, however, cannot seem to find a way to connect meaningfully to her family; she laments the fact that she feels as alienated from her son as he clearly feels from her and that her feelings for her husband Robbie resemble pity and resentment more than love. She cannot connect easily with her students either and carefully keeps personal details about her life completely out of the classroom. Finally, Janet comes to interpret Bellamy's long-ago intervention as a prescient warning:

"He'd seen how skilled she was, how coldly persuasive she could be; he'd known that she would use the study of literature to distance herself. Maybe he even foresaw how things would go for her and Robbie, how she'd win every argument in their marriage until the marriage was gone" (51).

Janet Moore fits in seamlessly with other academic characters featured in Russo's body of work. Like Hank Devereaux before her in *Straight Man* (1997) and Jack Griffin after her in *That Old Cape Magic* (2009), Janet suffers under the weight of impossible academic expectations. For Hank and Griffin, these expectations stem from the successful academic careers of their parents; for Janet, they arise from Bellamy, her adopted father figure. Yet Bellamy's comments doom her, like the rider in the poem, to gallop alone, in the dark, with no perceived destination. However the story, full of ominous refrains and melancholy sadness, ultimately ends on a considerably more positive note. Janet surprises herself by inviting a semiretired alcoholic colleague to her home on Thanksgiving and then decides to purge Bellamy's ghost from her consciousness once and for all by completing an academic reading assignment he had given her long ago—an assignment she now believes was meant to encourage her to "find that last elusive thing, a self worth being, worth becoming, and finally worth revealing" (55). It seems that the advice she wants to give her unrepentant plagiarizing student—that "he could find a better self" (49) if he wants to—is the advice that she herself finally absorbs. In the final moment of the story, Judith considers her future with a glimmer of genuine hope and enthusiasm: "Tonight they'd eat pizza. Tomorrow she'd find out what the hell mincemeat was. Then they'd celebrate Thanksgiving. After that, who knew?" (55).

Elsewhere (2012)

Published in late 2012, *Elsewhere* is an unusual memoir in that the story is equal parts the author's and his mother's. Jean Russo emerges in *Elsewhere* as both dominant and submissive, independent and dependent, at times her son's best friend and at other times his worst nightmare. Not until the end of the book does her diagnosis become clear; Jean Russo suffered tremendously from obsessive-compulsive disorder (OCD). Her symptoms manifested not in more common behaviors such as relentless hand washing or counting, but rather in her frequent need for reassurance and comfort, to an extent far beyond that required by most individuals. Richard Russo's posthumous, layman's diagnosis of his mother's OCD happened by way of his daughter's more recent diagnosis and his subsequent researching of the disorder. He admits sadly that "as dispiriting as it was to recognize my mother on virtually every page of the OCD book, it was even more painful to recognize myself as her principal enabler" (225). In sum, *Elsewhere* serves as a tender and honest chronicle of Russo's complicated relationship with his mother.

Readers familiar with Russo's work have long attempted to read his biography into his fiction; Gloversville, New York, is obviously the model for Mohawk, Thomaston, Empire Falls, and other worn-out Rust Belt towns that appear in his novels, and Russo has acknowledged that Dallas Younger in *Mohawk,* Sully in *Nobody's Fool,* Max Roby in *Empire Falls,* and, most of all, Sam Hall in *The Risk Pool* are all to some extent based on his own father. Jean Russo appears more obliquely in her son's novels; Russo commented in a 2012 interview that "Anne Grouse, in *Mohawk,* is my mother on a good day—brave, faithful, lovely, determined. Ned Hall's mother in *The Risk Pool* is the same woman on those days when the demons closed in— unhinged, terrified, needy, ill."[14] But while *The Risk Pool* explores many facets of Ned's and his mother's unstable relationship, the novel is more concerned, and more interested in, his relationship with his ne'er-do-well father, Sam. On the other hand, the personal stories in *Elsewhere* suggest that Russo's real-life father was much less of a presence in his life than Sam was in Ned's and that his mother was a much stronger and more indelible influence. Indeed in *The Risk Pool,* Ned begins to make his break from Mohawk when he enrolls at the University of Arizona at Tucson and points his dilapidated Ford Galaxie toward the Southwest and away from upstate New York. In real life, however, Jean Russo rode shotgun in that Galaxie's passenger seat, right alongside her son Richard, as the two of them together broke from Gloversville to try to remake their lives in Arizona.

Jean's efforts to leave Gloversville behind were never wholly successful, however, and she returned to her hometown on several occasions over the years to live, temporarily, with her parents or her sister. But for most of Russo's adult life, she lived near him, sometimes even in the same house, in Arizona, Pennsylvania, Illinois, Connecticut, and Maine. Unwilling to live for long without being close to the son whom she called "my rock," she relied on Russo for everything from grocery shopping and doctors' appointments to general company and, always, unstinting support. Russo packed and unpacked his mother's belongings countless times, not without complaint but always with the sense that this caretaker's role justifiably fell to him.

Russo is well known for his comic writing and his understated, humorous tone, but *Elsewhere* is far from a typical comic work. Still, the anecdotes he shares often shine with moments of dark, arid humor, such as his precollege road trip, his mother by his side, in an underpowered car dubbed "The Gray Death," which propelled them slowly from Gloversville to Tucson. Russo creates a noticeable narrative distance in telling the story of his relationship with his mother; even though, as a memoir, the voice is necessarily first-person, a space exists between the voice and the actual experience, a distance that serves to soften, at least a bit, much of the pain and stress of the experience. For example, not long after Russo's marriage to Barbara, Jean comes to live with the young couple in their single-wide trailer in Tucson. Jean has no job, no money, no prospects, and a strong dependence on Valium to mitigate her constant shaking. Clearly her presence in the trailer seriously taxes Russo's brand-new marriage, and he offers several examples of how Jean essentially ignored Barbara and how he and his wife would whisper together in bed in the only private conversations they could have. But Russo's tone is not condemning, or angry, or bitter, or even victimized. He could have made Jean seem worse than he does, or Barbara more selfless, or himself more beleaguered. Rather he treats the scene with a sort of detached objectivity, not indulging in self-pity or speculating on the feelings of others. "We dealt with it," he seems to say. And when the day finally comes when his mother moves out of their trailer and into her own apartment, Russo seems both surprised and grateful to find that "somehow there was still an 'us' for my wife and I to protect and cherish" (81).

Russo bookends *Elsewhere* with pieces repurposed from his long nonfiction essay titled "High and Dry," first published in *Granta* in 2010 and then republished as one of the four discretely bound works in *Interventions* (2012). *Elsewhere* begins with an expository prologue on Gloversville, its history, and how both his grandfathers happened to settle there in the early part of the twentieth century, drawn by what appeared to be a perpetually flourishing leather industry. Along the way Russo describes how he remembers downtown Gloversville when he was a boy in the 1950s, full of pedestrians busily hustling in and out of busy shops, movie theaters, bars, pool halls, and restaurants. By the time he graduated from high school in the late 1960s, though, the downtown seemed abandoned; cheap overseas labor had effectively strangled the domestic leather industry, and as factories and shops closed, jobs disappeared and Gloversville's economy collapsed. Leather workers endured longer layoffs and poorer working conditions; families such as the Russos were stretched tighter and tighter. Still, Russo acknowledges that as a boy, none of this had much effect on him (11); these observations belonged to his older self, the one looking back on his life in *Elsewhere*.

The book concludes with other segments culled from "High and Dry," interspersed with his own reflections on his mother's life, her undiagnosed illness, and the battle his younger daughter is now waging against her own OCD. The final moments of the memoir firmly position Russo in the present, looking back not only on his mother's life but also on the lives of his cousins and other relatives who still make their permanent homes in Gloversville. By the end he has come to a clearer understanding of his mother's experiences, her seemingly irrational obsessions, and his own complicity in her illness. He seems on the verge of forgiving himself for not understanding his mother better and acknowledges that his family "assures me I did everything that could've been done" (242), but the book closes with a moment of insecurity, of self-doubt, that he attributes to the irrevocable fact that he is "my mother's son" (243).

Widely reviewed upon its release, *Elsewhere* received mostly favorable comments. One critic from *Kirkus Reviews* noted that the memoir "contains much of the grace and flinty humor of [Russo's] fiction" and offers an "affecting yet never saccharine glimpse of the relationship among place, family and fiction."[15] Another reviewer, this one in the *Wall Street Journal,* commented, "The greatest charm of this memoir lies in the absence of self-pity and pretension in the author's take on his own history," and that finally, readers "can't help feeling that Jean must have done something right—that, even as she clung to her son like a barnacle, the laserlike intensity of this single mother's love for her only child was enough to turn him into an admirable adult."[16]

Nate in Venice (2013)

Nate in Venice was published on January 28, 2013, by Byliner exclusively in electronic format; it is currently available on the Byliner.com Web site, iTunes, and as an Amazon Kindle Single. When asked in a 2013 podcast interview about his foray into the world of e-publishing, especially after his resistance to creating an electronic version of *Interventions*, Russo replied that he has at times been misrepresented as someone completely against electronic books. One of Russo's goals for *Interventions* was for readers to have a strong, positive, tactile experience holding a beautifully bound book printed on especially high-quality paper; thus an electronic version of that work made little sense. But, Russo continued, the method of delivery— whether e-book or traditional print volume—is not nearly as important as the story itself, and electronic publishing is quickly becoming established as an important venue for contemporary fiction.[17]

Nate in Venice, a novella, is particularly well suited to electronic publishing, given that novella-length fiction is notoriously difficult to publish through conventional presses. Traditional publishing outlets exist for short stories of thirty-five pages or fewer, or novels of more than two hundred pages. But anything in between—what Russo calls the "dead zone"—does not fit the typical word-length requirements for either magazines or book publishers, and the typescript for *Nate in Venice,* which ran to about 125 pages, fell squarely within that dead zone. Electronic publishing, however, with its built-in flexibility, treats novellas no differently than any other genre of fiction; the number of pages of an e-book matters very little when the delivery is entirely digital. Because of this flexibility, Russo heralds electronic publishing as a potential savior of the novella and predicts that more writers will soon return to this almost-forgotten form—a form that he loves—since online magazines and other digital retail outlets are able to distribute them so easily.

Nate in Venice focuses on Nate Wilson, a sixty-something, newly retired English professor on a group tour to Italy to see the Biennale, an international contemporary art exhibit. Also on the tour are Nate's estranged brother, Julian, and several other colorful characters, including the elderly and nearly infirm Bernard and two sisters, Evelyn and Rene. The eleven short chapters in this novella, told by an omniscient third-person narrator, alternate between the present of the story, in Venice, and Nate's recent past. During the flashback chapters, readers gradually come to understand the traumatic event that led to Nate's abrupt retirement and the intense emotional distress he has experienced ever since. In *Nate in Venice*, Russo returns to several elements that appear in his previous works; for example, Venice, Russo's only international setting to date, also provides the backdrop in portions of *Bridge of Sighs*, and professors (or former professors) also regularly populate his fiction, including Peter Sullivan in *Nobody's Fool*, Hank Devereaux (and his parents) in *Straight Man* and "The Farther You Go," Jack Griffin (and his parents) in *That Old Cape Magic*, the narrator in "The Whore's Child," Paul Snow in "Buoyancy," and Janet Moore in "Horseman."

Nate in Venice also addresses another theme common to much of Russo's work: the insecurities and regrets that come with aging. In *Straight Man*, Hank Devereaux struggles to come to terms with his imminent fiftieth birthday, and in *That Old Cape Magic*, Jack Griffin wonders if he made the right decisions regarding his career path and his marriage. In *Nate in Venice*, Nate repeatedly ponders the question of whether he "led a life other than the one he was intended for." Like Russo himself, Nate once found himself at a crossroads in his life, when he faced the decision either to continue with his education or to pursue a life of honest manual labor. While he was a student, Nate had an apprenticeship with a contractor named Handscombe, who taught him not only the basics of carpentry, plumbing, and wiring but also the satisfaction that accompanies physical labor. But even though "the rhetorical tools he employed during the school year weren't nearly as satisfying as the more physical ones dangling from his tool belt in July and August,"

Nate, like Russo, chooses the life of the mind. Now, many years later and beginning his retirement, Nate questions the wisdom of his choice.

Over the course of the novella, Nate grapples with a mysterious issue introduced in the first paragraph: "what happened with the Mauntz girl." Readers come to learn that "the Mauntz girl" is Opal Mauntz, a brilliant college student suffering from an incapacitating and enigmatic disability that prevents her from speaking or coming close to anyone physically. The disability is described on the student health form she presents to Nate as "a problem with physical proximity," and the dean of liberal arts suggests that Opal may suffer from Asperger's syndrome. Nate, however, stubbornly resists these diagnoses and instead convinces himself that Opal simply needs a friend to open up to and that he is just the person to "make her understand that she was not alone."

Nate's obsession with Opal intensifies when her essays in his Jane Austen seminar demonstrate that she is a superb thinker and a dazzling writer, despite her silence during class and her physical isolation on the periphery of the room. He becomes increasingly determined to find a way to talk to her and to get her to speak, and so he hatches a well-meaning but disastrous exercise to share her writing with the class. In a bizarre and disturbing scene in which all seven of his "regular" students are roaring drunk and rubbing themselves with raw, greasy bacon, Opal arrives late to class, battered from an accident suffered on a piece of exercise equipment. Nate approaches Opal, believing that he is protecting her from the others, and reaches out to touch her bruised cheek. "Wasn't that what you were supposed to do with another human being in need?" he asks himself later. But touching the girl provokes "a keening yowl," and Nate realizes, too late, that he had made a terrible mistake in "confusing her need, her bewilderment, her inability to kick down life's barriers, with his own." As a result of this traumatizing incident, Opal leaves college for a mental hospital, and Nate is dismissed from his position.

Nate's academic specialization is Jane Austen, a writer who herself specializes, as Russo commented, in the "overlooked."[18] Yet Nate overlooks the healthy, whole people in his life—including, for a time, his fellow traveler Evelyn—because he is unfailingly drawn to "broken" people. Opal epitomizes this "brokenness," and through his interactions with her, Nate reveals his own overwhelming desire to fix and comfort those who seem somehow damaged or impaired. Furthermore he proves to be a maddeningly slow learner, for even after the shocking incident with Opal, Nate still finds himself irresistibly attracted to Rene. Her "paralyzing anxiety" functions like a peculiar but powerful aphrodisiac to Nate, and he immediately begins imagining a life with Rene that is "devoted to reassuring this lovely woman that there is absolutely nothing to fear."

The guilt that Nate feels for driving Opal over the edge deeply colors his experiences in Venice and drives his alarmingly low self-esteem, but he knows, as do readers, that deep down he is not a bad person. He is kind and generous—much more so than Julian, his hard and selfish brother, who skips out on the hotel bill (leaving it for Nate) and speaks cruelly to the fragile Rene. Julian is a salesman through and through and is all extroverted charisma and swagger and charm. Nate, on the other hand, lives in his own head most of the time and struggles to overcome his particular propensity to project his own fantasies onto others, imagining them as he wishes they were, which, of course, is inevitably much different from their real selves. Nevertheless, Nate does learn that he can make meaningful emotional connections; he helps the physically weakened Bernard, a man haunted by regrets, to scatter his late wife's ashes, and by the end of the story it seems that he may even have a future with Evelyn, who makes him feel "as if he'd been taken off a ventilator he hadn't even known he was on, able once again to fill his lungs on his own." The story concludes with a feeling of hope for the future; Nate believes that he will finally be able to clear the air with his brother and truly communicate with him—something he has wanted to do for years. Although Nate's ultimate conclusion is that "life is, seemingly by design, a botched job," he realizes that this does not mean that happiness is impossible but rather that one must acknowledge one's failings honestly and then move on without giving up. Nate's richly internal, retrospective point of view represents Russo's ever-deepening engagement with the complicated and sometimes painful process of reckoning honestly with the past.

Screenwriting

Along with his accomplished career as a fiction writer, Russo has enjoyed considerable success as a screenwriter. He wrote or cowrote the screenplays for such films as *Twilight* (1998), *The Flamingo Rising* (2001), *The Ice Harvest* (2005), and *Keeping Mum* (2005) and the HBO miniseries *Empire Falls* (2005). When asked in a 2010 interview about his experiences writing screenplays, Russo explained that he enjoys screenwriting because it "plays right into my strengths, because most screenplays are about dialogue, which comes easiest for me. The other thing about screenplays—they're action heavy. You put characters in motion and let them talk and behave in ways that reveal their inner life, and those are the two things that, for me, are easiest to do."[19] In his first foray into screenwriting, he collaborated with Robert Benton on the screenplay for *Nobody's Fool* (1994); the pair reunited to write the screenplay for the murder mystery *Twilight*. Russo described this collaboration as unlike anything he had ever experienced as a writer. "When we got about a hundred pages into this detective movie," Russo recalled, "neither of us knew who had committed the murder, and we were twenty pages from the end of the script. So we went backward and just decided, All right, here's the guy who committed the murder. . . . And then we worked backward and rewrote the screenplay the same way. Even as I tell that story, it's astonishing to me that the movie could possibly have been made working in that lunatic way."[20]

Russo continues to work on screenplays and recently completed a draft adaptation of Bill Bryson's *A Walk in the Woods*, which has yet to go into production. Nevertheless, despite the success that he has enjoyed as a screenwriter, Russo believes that his primary calling is as a novelist. At this writing Russo is working on a sequel to *Nobody's Fool*, which returns to the town of North Bath and takes as its focus not Sully but rather the hapless police officer Doug Raymer, who has a series of run-ins with Sully in the first novel. The novel is tentatively titled *Everybody's Fool*.

NOTES

Chapter 1—Understanding Richard Russo

1. Birnbaum, "Richard Russo."
2. Paul Grondahl, "Russo Returns to Upstate Pride and Paradox," *Albany (N.Y.) Times Union*, September 30, 2007, http://blog.timesunion.com/localarts/russo-returns-to-upstate-pride-and-paradox/1135/ (accessed May 27, 2013).
3. Russo, "High and Dry," 215.
4. Ibid., 229.
5. Ibid., 207.
6. Ibid., 213.
7. Russo, *Elsewhere*, 209.
8. Russo, "High and Dry," 222.
9. James Richard Russo, "The Craft of Charles Brockden Brown's Fiction" (Ph.D. diss., University of Arizona, 1979).
10. Edmonds et al., "A Conversation," 91.
11. Russo, *Elsewhere*, 87.
12. John Marshall, "Pulitzer Prize Winner Richard Russo Is an Open Book about His Work," *Seattle Post-Intelligencer*, September 11, 2008, http://www.seattlepi.com/default/article/Pulitzer-Prize-winner-Richard-Russo-is-an-open-1284912.php (accessed May 27, 2013).
13. Erin McGraw, "Surface Tension," *Southern Review* 40:2 (Spring 2004): 384–401.
14. Rosen, "New Russo Collaboration."
15. Ibid.
16. Edmonds et al., "A Conversation," 93.
17. Ibid., 92.
18. Russo, "Introduction: Secret Hearts," xx.
19. Birnbaum, "Richard Russo."
20. "Meet the Writers: Richard Russo," *BarnesandNoble.com*, Spring 2005, http://www.barnesandnoble.com/writers/writerdetails.asp?cid=968838 (accessed May 27, 2013).
21. Dollacker, "An Interview with Richard Russo: Part 1."
22. "Meet the Writers."
23. Russo, "In Defense of Omniscience," 17.
24. Ibid., 16.
25. Dollacker, "An Interview with Richard Russo: Part 1."
26. Ibid.

27. "Interview with Richard Russo," *Failbetter.com.*

28. Ibid.

29. Justin Mason, "Downtrodden Gloversville an Inspiration to Author Richard Russo," *Schenectady (N.Y.) Daily Gazette,* February 24, 2012, http://www.dailygazette .com/news/2012/feb/24/0224_russo/ (accessed May 27, 2013).

Chapter 2—*Mohawk*

1. Smith, "Richard Russo: The Novelist Again," 43.

2. Dollacker, "An Interview with Richard Russo: Part 1."

3. "*Mohawk,*" *Kirkus Reviews,* August 15, 1986, https://www.kirkusreviews.com/ book-reviews/richard-russo/mohawk/#review (accessed May 27, 2013).

4. Greg Johnson, "In Short: Fiction," *New York Times,* October 12, 1986, http:// www.nytimes.com/books/01/06/24/specials/russo-mohawk.html (accessed May 27, 2013).

5. Such critics include but are not limited to Michiko Kakutani and Greg Johnson, both of the *New York Times,* and David Montrose of the *Times Literary Supplement.*

6. Michiko Kakutani, "Books of the Times: *Mohawk,*" *New York Times,* October 15, 1986, C24.

Chapter 3—*The Risk Pool*

1. Michiko Kakutani, "Growing Up 'Pretty Near the Edge,'" *New York Times,* November 2, 1988, C25.

2. Jack Sullivan, "'Things Get Bad,' Says Dad," *New York Times Book Review,* December 18, 1988, 14.

3. "Review," *Library Journal,* November 15, 1988, 86.

4. Sullivan, "Things Get Bad," 14.

Chapter 4—*Nobody's Fool*

1. Smith, "Richard Russo: The Novelist Again," 43.

2. Ibid.

3. Francine Prose, "Small Town Smart Alecks," *New York Times,* June 20, 1993, BR13.

4. John Skow, "Boarded Up Glocca Morra," *Time* 141:22 (May 31, 1993): 66.

5. Steve Brzezinski, review of *Nobody's Fool, Antioch Review* 52:1 (Winter 1994): 173.

6. Zachary Leader, "Pretty, Green Graves," *Times Literary Supplement* 4709 (July 2, 1993): 23.

7. Smith, "Richard Russo: The Novelist Again," 43.

8. Edmonds et al., "A Conversation," 96.

Chapter 5—*Straight Man*

1. Russo, "How 'I' Moved Heaven and Earth," 85.

2. Weich, "Richard Russo's Working Arrangements."

3. Leuschner, "Body Damage," 345.

4. Elaine Showalter, *Faculty Towers: The Academic Novel and Its Discontents* (Philadelphia: University of Pennsylvania Press, 2005), 88.

5. Tom De Haven, "Screwball U," review of *Straight Man* by Richard Russo, *New York Times,* July 6, 1997, BR10.

6. Review of *Straight Man* by Richard Russo, *Publishers Weekly*, May 12, 1997, 56.

7. Ron Charles, "Pillorying Pretentious Professors," *Christian Science Monitor* 89:218 (1997): 14.

8. Rita D. Jacobs, review of *Straight Man* by Richard Russo, *World Literature Today* 72:4 (Autumn 1998): 832–33.

9. Michael Lee, "Russo Blends a Deft Comic Touch with Heavy Philosophical Lifting," *National Catholic Reporter*, September 26, 1997, 33.

10. Frumkes, "A Conversation with Richard Russo."

11. The episode in the novel that includes threatening to kill "a duck a day" is based on a real conversation Russo had with a dean at Penn State–Altoona when Russo was a faculty member there.

12. Leuschner, "Body Damage," 340.

13. Cirisi, "Straight Men and Other Ordinary Joes," 44.

14. Costa, Review of *Straight Man*, 746.

15. This story was originally published in a slightly different form as a short story titled simply "Dog" in the December 23–30, 1996, issue of the *New Yorker*.

16. Janice Rossen, *The University in Modern Fiction: When Power Is Academic* (New York: St. Martin's Press, 1993), 188.

17. De Haven, "Screwball U," BR10.

Chapter 6 — Empire Falls

1. Bob Minzesheimer, "The Book Club's First Pick: Russo's 'Empire Falls' Portrait," *USA Today*, February 21, 2012, 7d.

2. "A Conversation with Richard Russo," *Random House "About the Author" Interview*, http://www.randomhouse.com/knopf/authors/russo/qna.html (accessed May 30, 2013).

3. Gary Levin, "'Empire Falls' Overflows with Big Cast, Story," *USA Today*, May 26, 2005. g. 03d.

4. Russo's novella *Intervention* (2012) is also set in Maine.

5. Peter Smith, "Richard Russo."

6. Mudge, "Richard Russo."

7. Ibid.

8. "A Conversation with Richard Russo," *Random House "About the Author" Interview*.

9. "Interview with Richard Russo," *Failbetter.com*.

10. Farnsworth, "Pulitzer Prize Winner."

11. Ibid.

12. Birnbaum, "Richard Russo."

13. Farnsworth, "Pulitzer Prize Winner."

14. Scott, "Townies."

15. "A Conversation with Richard Russo, Author of *Empire Falls*," *BookBrowse.com*, 2001, http://www.bookbrowse.com/author_interviews/full/index.cfm/author_number/618/richard-russo (accessed May 30, 2013).

16. "Threadbare," *Economist* 359:8223 (May 26, 2001–June 1, 2001): 87.

17. Janet Maslin, "Turning against the Tide in a Backwater," *New York Times*, May 10, 2001, 9.

18. Review of *Empire Falls*, *Library Journal*, July 1, 2001, 126.

19. "*HBR*'s Best Business Books of 2001," *Harvard Business Review* 87:5 (May 2009): 106–7.

20. Scott, "Townies."

Chapter 7—*Bridge of Sighs*

1. "Bridge of Sighs," *Kirkus Reviews* 75:15 (August 1, 2007): 10–11.

2. Joanne Wilkinson, "Bridge of Sighs," *Booklist*, September 1, 2007, 5.

3. Christopher Borrelli, "In Richard Russo's Novel, Nobody Leaves Their Comfort Zone," *Toledo (Ohio) Blade,* November 11, 2007, http://www.toledoblade.com/Books/2007/11/11/In-Richard-Russo-s-novel-nobody-leaves-their-comfort-zone.html (accessed May 30, 2013).

4. Michael Janairo, "Richard Russo Turns to Nonfiction to Tangle with the Legacy of His Hometown," August 22, 2010, *TimesUnion.com* (Albany, N.Y.), http://www.timesunion.com/default/article/Richard-Russo-turns-to-nonfiction-to-tangle-with-625398.php (accessed May 27, 2013).

5. "Richard Russo's Small-Town America," interview with Steve Inskeep, Morning Edition, National Public Radio, October 1, 2007.

6. "Bridge of Sighs," *Kirkus Reviews* 75:15 (August 1, 2007): 10–11.

7. Edmonds et al., "A Conversation," 101–2.

8. Ibid., 99.

9. Wilkinson, "Bridge of Sighs," 5.

10. "Bridge of Sighs," *Kirkus Reviews* 75:18 (September 15, 2007): 957–58.

11. Bob Minzesheimer, "In 'Bridge of Sighs,' Small Town Opens Window to a Big World," *USA Today,* August 25, 2007, 4d.

12. Jeffrey Frank, "Bridge of Sighs," *Publishers Weekly,* August 13, 2007, 40.

13. Stephen Amidon, "Old Dog, Old Tricks," *London Sunday Times,* October 28, 2007, 54.

14. Louis Menand, "Upstate," *New Yorker* 83:31 (October 15, 2007): 100–101.

15. Daniel M. Murtagh, "An Art of Dislocation," *Commonweal,* March 28, 2008, 24.

16. Frank Campbell, "Master of Home Truths," *Australian,* November 17, 2007, http://www.news.com.au/news/master-of-home-truths/story-fna7dq6e-1111114866291 (accessed May 27, 2013).

17. Edmonds et al., "A Conversation," 107.

Chapter 8—*That Old Cape Magic*

1. Allen, "A Matter of Inheritance," 26–27.

2. Griffin's wife Joy is aptly named, even though she appears to have little enough joy in her life as she deals with her self-deluded husband. She is one of several Russo characters whose names evoke aspects of their natures, including Grace Roby in *Empire Falls.*

3. This moment when a lonely child adopts another whole family recalls Sarah Berg's feelings toward the whole Lynch family in *Bridge of Sighs.*

4. Allen, "A Matter of Inheritance," 27.

5. Bush, "That Old Cape Magic," 42.

6. Ibid., 41.

7. Sally Bissell, "That Old Cape Magic," *Library Journal,* August 15, 2009, 74.

8. Deborah J. Knuth Klenck, "Mixed Up in Maine," *America,* December 7, 2009, 25–26.

Chapter 9—Other Works

1. Rand Richards Cooper, "Bitter Harvests," *New York Times,* July 14, 2002, F10.

2. Eugenia Williamson, "Richard Russo Chosen for One City, One Story," *Phoenix,* June 20, 2011, http://blog.thephoenix.com/blogs/pageviews/archive/2011/06/20/richard-russo-chosen-for-one-city-one-story.aspx (accessed May 29, 2013).

3. Birnbaum, "Richard Russo on *The Whore's Child.*"

4. Tom Deignan, "Good Liars," *World & I* 17:11 (November 2002): 229–33.

5. Francine Prose, review, "*The Whore's Child and Other Stories*," *People* 58:4 (July 22, 2002): 35.

6. Peter Heinegg, "You *Still* Can't Get There from Here," *America,* October 21, 2002, 26–27.

7. Birnbaum, "Richard Russo on *The Whore's Child.*"

8. Cooper, "Bitter Harvests."

9. Steve Rosenbaum, "Independent Booksellers Have Never Faced Anything Like Amazon," *Huffington Post,* May 25, 2012, http://www.huffingtonpost.com/steve-rosenbaum/whos-blowin-who-asks-ron_b_1545699.html (accessed May 29, 2013).

10. Martin Chilton, "Richard Russo Novel Not for Sale as e-book," *London (U.K.) Telegraph,* June 25, 2012, http://www.telegraph.co.uk/culture/books/booknews/9354365/Richard-Russo-novel-not-for-sale-as-e-book.html (accessed May 30, 2013).

11. Ibid.

12. Russo, *Elsewhere,* 228.

13. Edmonds et al., "A Conversation," 103–4.

14. Williams, "Mother and Son."

15. "Elsewhere: A Memoir," *Kirkus Reviews* 80:18 (November 5, 2012): 313.

16. Finnerty, "A Look Back," A15.

17. Usery, "Richard Russo's New Novella."

18. Ibid.

19. Edmonds et al., "A Conversation," 93.

20. Ibid., 94–95.

SELECTED BIBLIOGRAPHY

Works by Richard Russo

BOOKS

Mohawk. New York: Random House, 1986.
The Risk Pool. New York: Random House, 1988.
Nobody's Fool. New York: Random House, 1993.
Straight Man. New York: Random House, 1997.
Empire Falls. New York: Random House, 2001.
The Whore's Child and Other Stories. New York: Random House, 2002.
Bridge of Sighs. New York: Random House, 2007.
A Healing Touch: True Stories of Life, Death, and Hospice, ed. Richard Russo. Camden, Maine: Down East Books, 2008.
That Old Cape Magic. New York: Random House, 2009.
Interventions: A Novella & Three Stories. Camden, Maine: Down East Books, 2012.
Elsewhere: A Memoir. New York: Random House, 2012.

SHORT STORIES, ESSAYS, AND NOVELLAS

"The Top of the Tree." *Mid-American Review* 1:1 (Fall 1981): 113–29.
"The Dowry." *Prairie Schooner* 59:3 (Fall 1985): 3–25.
"Fishing with Wussy." *Granta* 19 (Summer 1986). http://www.granta.com/Archive/19/Fishing-with-Wussy/Page-1 (accessed May 28, 2013).
"Dog." *New Yorker,* December 23, 1996, 74–75, 78–79.
"Horseman." *Atlantic* (August 1, 2006). http://www.theatlantic.com/magazine/archive/2006/08/horseman/305039/ (accessed May 30, 2013).
"High and Dry." *Granta* 111 (Summer 2010): 204–30.
Nate in Venice. Byliner.com, January 28, 2013. https://www.byliner.com/originals/nate-in-venice?hbl (accessed May 28, 2013).

CONTRIBUTIONS TO OTHER VOLUMES

"Pork." In *We Are What We Ate: 24 Memories of Food,* edited by Mark Winegardner, 191–200. New York: Harcourt Brace, 1998.
"Location, Location, Location: Depicting Character through Place." In *Creating Fiction: Instruction and Insights from Teachers of the Associated Writing Programs,* edited by Julie Checkoway, 67–80. Cincinnati, Ohio: Story Press, 1999.
"Autumn." In *Maine: The Seasons,* edited by Terrill S. Lester, 67–71. New York: Knopf, 2001.

"In Defense of Omniscience." In *Bringing the Devil to His Knees: The Craft of Fiction and the Writing Life*, edited by Charles Baxter and Peter Turchi, 7–17. Ann Arbor: University of Michigan Press, 2001.

"Surf and Turf." In *Death by Pad Thai and Other Unforgettable Meals*, edited by Douglas Bauer, 98–104. New York: Three Rivers Press, 2006.

INTRODUCTIONS, FOREWORDS, AND AFTERWORDS

"Introduction: Secret Hearts." In *The Collected Stories of Richard Yates*, xi–xx. New York: Henry Holt, 2001.

"Afterword: Imagining Jenny." In *She's Not There: A Life in Two Genders*, by Jennifer Finney Boylan, 279–300. New York: Broadway Books, 2003.

Foreword. In *Bottom of the Ninth: Great Contemporary Baseball Short Stories*, edited and with an introduction by John McNally, xi–xii. Carbondale and Edwardsville: Southern Illinois University Press, 2003.

Introduction. In *The Story Behind the Story: 26 Stories by Contemporary Writers and How They Work*, edited by Peter Turchi and Andrea Barrett, 9–15. New York: W. W. Norton, 2004.

Introduction. In *The Best American Short Stories 2010, Selected from U.S. and Canadian Magazines*, edited by Richard Russo with Heidi Pitlor, xiii–xix. Boston and New York: Houghton Mifflin Harcourt, 2010.

Introduction. In *My Bookstore: Writers Celebrate Their Favorite Places to Browse, Read, and Shop*, edited by Ronald Rice and Booksellers across America, xi–xiv. New York: Black Dog & Leventhal, 2012.

SCREENPLAYS AND TELEPLAYS

Twilight. Screenplay by Richard Russo and Robert Benton. Paramount Pictures, 1998.

The Flamingo Rising. Teleplay by Richard Russo. Hallmark Hall of Fame Productions, 2001.

Brush with Fate. Teleplay by Richard Russo. Hallmark Hall of Fame Productions, 2003.

Empire Falls. Novel and teleplay by Richard Russo. HBO Films, 2005.

The Ice Harvest. Screenplay by Richard Russo and Robert Benton. Focus Features, 2005.

Keeping Mum. Story by Richard Russo. Screenplay by Richard Russo and Niall Johnson. Summit Entertainment, 2005.

SELECTED ARTICLES

"How 'I' Moved Heaven and Earth." *New York Times Magazine*, October 17, 1999, 85.

"Amazon's Jungle Logic." Op-ed, *New York Times*, December 12, 2001, A35.

"Mankind Is Our Business." *Publishers Weekly*, March 3, 2008, 52.

"Redefining Laziness." *Powells.com Original Essays*. http://www.powells.com/essays/russo.html (accessed May 28, 2013).

Works about Richard Russo

INTERVIEWS AND PROFILES

Birnbaum, Robert. "Richard Russo." *Identity Theory*, June 16, 2001. http://www.identitytheory.com/richard-russo/ (accessed May 28, 2013).

Birnbaum, Robert. "Richard Russo on *The Whore's Child.*" *Identity Theory*, August 11, 2002. http://www.identitytheory.com/richard-russo-the-whores-child/ (accessed May 29, 2013).

Chang, Jade. "Interview with Richard Russo." *Goodreads.com*, November 2012. http://www.goodreads.com/interviews/show/818.Richard_Russo (accessed May 27, 2013).

Craigo, Karen. "At the Camden Deli: Editor Karen Craigo Interviews Pulitzer Prize–Winner and Former *MAR* Contributor Richard Russo on His Home Turf." *Mid-American Review* 25:1 (2004): 208–17.

Dollacker, Sarah Sacha. "An Interview with Richard Russo: Part 1." *Red Room Library*, November 5, 2009. http://www.redroomlibrary.com/2009/11/interview-with-richard-russo-part-1.html (accessed May 27, 2013).

Edmonds, Sam, Laura Ender, and Brendan Lynaugh. "A Conversation with Richard Russo, April 17, 2010." *Willow Springs* 68 (Fall 2011): 90–107.

Farnsworth, Elizabeth. "Pulitzer Prize Winner: Fiction." *Online NewsHour*, May 7, 2002. http://www.pbs.org/newshour/conversation/jan-june02/russo_5–07.html (accessed May 27, 2013).

Frumkes, Lewis Burke. "A Conversation with Richard Russo." *Writer* 113:12 (December 2000): 19–21.

Holt, Karen. "Writing What He Knows." *Publishers Weekly*, August 27, 2007, 43–44.

"Interview with Richard Russo." *Failbetter.com.* 2:3 (Summer/Fall 2001). http://failbetter.com/04/Russo.htm (accessed May 28, 2013).

"Interview with Richard Russo." In *Redivider: A Journal of New Literature and Art*, Emerson College, July 8, 2008. http://www.redividerjournal.org/interview-with-richard-russo/ (accessed May 29, 2013).

Interview with Richard Russo. In *Scout, Atticus, and Boo: A Celebration of Fifty Years of* To Kill a Mockingbird, edited by Mary McDonagh Murphy, 167–71. New York: HarperCollins, 2010.

Interview with Richard Russo. In *Writing for Your Life* #2, ed. Sybil Steinberg, 240–45. New York: W. W. Norton, 1995.

Jakamides, Annaliese. "Shhh, It's Russo." *BangorMetro.com*, September 1, 2009. http://www.bangormetro.com/item/151-shhh-its-russo (accessed May 28, 2013).

McGarvey, Bill. "Busted: Richard Russo." *Busted Halo*, November 6, 2007. http://bustedhalo.com/features/busted-richard-russo (accessed May 29, 2013).

Mudge, Alden. "Richard Russo Renders Timely Portrait of American Life." *BookPage.com*, May 2001. http://bookpage.com/interview/richard-russo-renders-timely-portrait-of-american-life (accessed May 27, 2013).

Smith, Peter. "Richard Russo." *Maine* (June 2010). http://themainemag.com/people/profiles/1310-richard-russo.html (accessed May 27, 2013).

Smith, Wendy. "Richard Russo: The Novelist Again Explores the Crucial Impact of Place on Individual Destinies." *Publishers Weekly* 240 (June 7, 1993): 43–44.

Weber, Bruce. "Richard Russo, Happily at Home in Winesburg East." *New York Times*, July 2, 2004. http://www.nytimes.com/2004/07/02/books/richard-russo-happily-at-home-in-winesburg-east.html?pagewanted=all&src=pm (accessed May 28, 2013).

Weich, Dave. "Richard Russo's Working Arrangements." *Powell's.com Interviews*, June 6, 2001. http://www.powells.com/blog/interviews/richard-russos-working-arrangements-by-dave/ (accessed May 28, 2013).

Williamson, Eugenia. "A Conversation between Richard Russo and Andre Dubus III: Blue Collar Poetry." *Portland Phoenix,* October 12, 2011. http://portland.thephoenix.com/arts/128260-conversation-between-richard-russo-and-andre-dub/?page=1#TOPCONTENT (accessed May 29, 2013).

Usery, Stephen. "Richard Russo's New Novella Is a Haunted—and Haunting—Tale of Regret and Loss." In *Chapter 16: A Community of Tennessee Writers, Readers, and Passersby.* Podcast. http://www.chapter16.org/content/russo-usery-interview (accessed May 29, 2013).

CRITICAL ANALYSES AND REVIEWS

"Academic Struggles to Find a Place in Today's World." *Journal of Popular Culture* 41:4 (2008): 591–600.

Allen, Brooke. "A Matter of Inheritance." *New Leader* (May/June–July/August 2009): 26–27.

Bush, Trudy. "That Old Cape Magic." *Christian Century,* December 15, 2009, 41–42.

Cirisi, Rita. "Straight Men and Other Ordinary Joes: An Introduction to Richard Russo." *Italian Americana* 18:1 (Winter 2000): 43–46.

Costa, Richard Hauer. Review of *Straight Man,* by Richard Russo. In *Magill's Literary Annual: 1998, Volume 2,* 745–49. Englewood Cliffs, N.J.: Salem Press, 1998.

Dalton-Brown, Sally. "Is There Life Outside of (the Genre of) the Campus Novel? The Academic Struggles to Find a Place in Today's World." *Journal of Popular Culture* 41:4 (2008): 591–600.

Denton, Stacy. "Nostalgia, Class and Rurality in *Empire Falls.*" *Journal of American Studies* 45:3 (2011): 503–18.

D'Haen, Theo. "The Return of History and the Minorization of New York: T. Coraghessen Boyle and Richard Russo." *Revue française d'études américaines* 62 (November 1994): 393–403.

Finnerty, Amy. "A Look Back, without Anger." *Wall Street Journal,* November 1, 2012, A15.

Furnish, Shearle. "Decay and Obsolescence in the Novels of Richard Russo." *CCTE Studies* 66 (2001): 30–36.

Hower, Edward, and Susan B. Reno. "Small-Town Dreams." *World & I* 16:10 (2001): 243.

Leuschner, Eric. "Body Damage: Dis-Figuring the Academic in Academic Fiction." *Review of Education, Pedagogy, and Cultural Studies* 28 (2006): 339–54.

Pastoor, Charles. "Divine Trickery, Long Shots, and Redemption in Richard Russo's *Nobody's Fool.*" *Intégrité: A Faith and Learning Journal* 10:1 (Spring 2011): 3–9.

"Richard Russo." *Contemporary Literary Criticism* 181. Gale Cengage Learning (2004): 228–71.

Rosen, Judith. "New Russo Collaboration is Print Only." *Publishers Weekly,* April 9, 2012. http://publishersweekly.com/pn/by-topic/industry-news/publisher-news/article/51422-new-russo-collaboration-is-print-only.html. (accessed January 4, 2014).

Scott, A. O. "Townies." *New York Times,* June 24, 2001. http://www.nytimes.com/books/01/06/24/reviews/010624.24scottt.html (accessed May 29, 2013).

Scott, Robert F. "It's a Small World, After All: Assessing the Contemporary Campus Novel." *Journal of the Midwest Modern Language Association* 31:1 (Spring 2004): 81–87.

Sheldon, Glenn. "Bust, Boom, and the American Diner in Russo's *Empire Falls.*" *CEA Critic* 69:1–2 (Fall 2006–Winter 2007): 86–92.

Tierney, William G. "Academic Freedom and Tenure: Between Fiction and Reality." *Journal of Higher Education* 75:2 (March/April 2004): 161–77.

Williams, John. "Mother and Son: Richard Russo Talks about 'Elsewhere.'" *New York Times,* October 30, 2012. http://artsbeat.blogs.nytimes.com/2012/10/30/mother -and-son-richard-russo-talks-about-elsewhere/ (accessed May 29, 2013).

INDEX

ABOUT THE AUTHOR

KATHLEEN DROWNE is an associate professor of American literature at Missouri University of Science and Technology in Rolla. She is the author or coauthor of several books, including *Spirits of Defiance: National Prohibition and Jazz Age Literature, 1920–1930* and *The 1920s: American Popular Culture through History*.